A Survival Guide for College Managers and Leaders

David Collins

continuum
LONDON • NEW YORK

Illustrations by Joanna Arthur

Continuum International Publishing Group
The Tower Building   80 Maiden Lane
11 York Road   Suite 704
London   New York
SE1 7NX   NY 10038

www.continuumbooks.com

British Library Cataloguing-in-Publication Data
A catalogue record for this book is available from the British Library.

ISBN: 0–8264–9081–6 (paperback)

Library of Congress Cataloging-in-Publication Data
A catalog record for this book is available from the Library of Congress.

Typeset by YHT Ltd
Printed and bound in Great Britain by MPG Books Ltd, Bodmin, Cornwall

Contents

The author

David Collins CBE MA PhD FRSA is currently Principal/ Chief Executive of South Cheshire College, which in 2004 received the best ever college inspection report with thirteen grades of 'Outstanding', including one for leadership and management. In 2006 it was also named as one of the 100 best companies to work for. His previous experience includes being the Vice Principal of Sandwell College where he developed the ISO 9000 quality assurance standard for colleges; a Head of Department at Redditch College (now North East Worcestershire College); and the Education Coordinator at Edinburgh Prison, Edinburgh Young Offenders. He has also acted in interim support roles to five other colleges in recovery situations as well as spending a year as acting Principal at what is now Bolton Community College. His main academic interests centre around the improvement of quality in Further Education and he has presented papers on various aspects of this topic in America, Australasia, Asia and South Africa, as well as in the United Kingdom. Dr Collins has served on a number of national advisory committees, including the 'Success for All' and 'Agenda for Change' implementation groups. More recently he has been involved with the Centre for Excellence in Leadership, leading SWOT teams into various colleges and designing and delivering the national Induction Programme for New Principals. David Collins is a Visiting Professorial Fellow at Lancaster University and was made a CBE in the Queen's birthday honours in 2005 for services to Further Education.

Series foreword

THE ESSENTIAL FE TOOLKIT SERIES

Jill Jameson
Series Editor

In the autumn of 1974, a young woman newly arrived from Africa landed in Devon to embark on a new life in England. Having travelled half way round the world, she still longed for sunny Zimbabwe. Not sure what career to follow, she took a part-time job teaching EFL to Finnish students. Having enjoyed this, she studied thereafter for a PGCE at the University of Nottingham in Ted Wragg's Education Department. After teaching in secondary schools, she returned to university in Cambridge, and, after graduating, took a job in ILEA in 1984 in adult education. She loved it: there was something about adult education that woke her up, made her feel fully alive, newly aware of all the lifelong learning journeys being followed by so many students and staff around her. The adult community centre she worked in was a joyful place for diverse multi-ethnic communities. Everyone was cared for, including 90-year-olds in wheelchairs, toddlers in the crèche, ESOL refugees, city accountants in business suits and university level graphic design students. In her eyes, the centre was an educational ideal, a remarkable place in which, gradually, everyone was helped to learn to be who they wanted to be. This was the Chequer Centre, Finsbury, EC1, the 'red house', as her daughter saw it, toddling in from the crèche. And so began the story of a long interest in further education that was to last for many years . . . why, if they did such good work for so many, were FE centres so under-funded and unrecognized, so under-appreciated?

It is with delight that, 32 years after the above story began, I write the Foreword to *The Essential FE Toolkit*, Continuum's new series of 24 books on further education (FE) for teachers and college leaders. The idea behind the *Toolkit* is to provide a

comprehensive guide to FE in a series of compact, readable
books. The suite of 24 individual books are gathered together
to provide the practitioner with an overall FE toolkit in specialist, fact-filled volumes designed to be easily accessible,
written by experts with significant knowledge and experience
in their individual fields. All of the authors have in-depth
understanding of further education. But 'Why is further education important? Why does it merit a whole series to be
written about it?' you may ask.

At the Association of Colleges Annual Conference in 2005, in
a humorous speech to college principals, John Brennan said that,
whereas in 1995 further education was a 'political backwater',
by 2005 it had become 'mainstream'. John recalled that since
1995 there had been '36 separate Government or Government-
sponsored reports or white papers specifically devoted to the
post-16 sector'. In our recent regional research report (2006) for
the Learning and Skills Development Agency, my co-author
Yvonne Hillier and I noted that it was no longer 'raining policy'
in FE, as we had described earlier (Jameson and Hillier, 2003):
there is now a torrent of new initiatives. We thought in 2003
that an umbrella would suffice to protect you. We'd now
recommend buying a boat to navigate these choppy waters, as it
looks as if John Brennan's 'mainstream' FE, combined with a
tidal wave of government policies will soon lead to a flood of
new interest in the sector, rather than end anytime soon.

There are good reasons for all this government attention on
further education. In 2004/2005, student numbers in LSC-
funded further education increased to 4.2m, total college
income was around £6.1 billion, and the average college had
an annual turnover of £15m. Further education has rapidly
increased in national significance regarding the need for ever
greater achievements in UK education and skills training for
millions of learners, providing qualifications and workforce
training to feed a UK national economy hungrily in competition with other OECD nations. The 120 recommendations of
the Foster Review (2005) therefore in the main encourage
colleges to focus their work on vocational skills, social inclusion
and achieving academic progress. This series is here to consider
all three of these areas and more.

The series is written for teaching practitioners, leaders and managers in the 572 FE/LSC-funded institutions in the UK, including FE colleges, adult education and sixth form institutions, prison education departments, training and workforce development units, local education authorities and community agencies. The series is also written for PGCE/Cert Ed/City & Guilds Initial and continuing professional development (CPD) teacher trainees in universities in the UK, USA, Canada, Australia, New Zealand and beyond. It will also be of interest to staff in the 600 Jobcentre Plus providers in the UK and to many private training organisations. All may find this series of use and interest in learning about FE educational practice in the 24 different areas of these specialist books from experts in the field.

Our use of this somewhat fuzzy term 'practitioners' includes staff in the FE/LSC-funded sector who engage in professional practice in governance, leadership, management, teaching, training, financial and administration services, student support services, ICT and MIS technical support, librarianship, learning resources, marketing, research and development, nursery and crèche services, community and business support, transport and estates management. It is also intended to include staff in a host of other FE services including work-related training, catering, outreach and specialist health, diagnostic additional learning support, pastoral and religious support for students. Updating staff in professional practice is critically important at a time of such continuing radical policy-driven change, and we are pleased to contribute to this nationally and internationally.

We are also privileged to have an exceptional range of authors writing for the series. Many of our series authors are renowned for their work in further education, having worked in the sector for thirty years or more. Some have received OBE or CBE honours, professorships, fellowships and awards for contributions they have made to further education. All have demonstrated a commitment to FE that makes their books come alive with a kind of wise guidance for the reader. Sometimes this is tinged with world-weariness, sometimes with sympathy, humour or excitement. Sometimes the books are just plain clever or a fascinating read, to guide practitioners of the future who will read these works. Together, the books make up a considerable portfolio of assets for you to take with you through your journeys in further education. We hope the experience of reading the books will be interesting, instructive and pleasurable and that experience gained from them will last, renewed, for many seasons.

It has been wonderful to work with all of the authors and with Continuum's UK Education Publisher, Alexandra Webster, on this series. The exhilarating opportunity of developing such a comprehensive toolkit of books probably comes once in a lifetime, if at all. I am privileged to have had this rare opportunity, and I thank the publishers, authors and other contributors to the series for making these books come to life with their fantastic contributions to FE.

Dr Jill Jameson
Series Editor
March, 2006

Series Editor's introduction

At the end of this stunning new book on college leadership, David Collins writes,

> If once in a lifetime someone came up to you and said, 'Thanks to you I am now doing things that I didn't dream I was capable of. You've changed my life', what an achievement that would be. In a college it's an everyday occurrence. Remember above everything else – you are the difference maker.' (David Collins 2006: 120)

This is a book for those who want to be 'difference makers'. A *Survival Guide for College Managers and Leaders* is written for *The Essential FE Toolkit* series by Dr David Collins CBE, MA, Ph.D, FRSA, Principal/Chief Executive of South Cheshire College. In 2004, South Cheshire College received the best ever college inspection report with thirteen grades of 'Outstanding', including one for leadership and management. In 2006 the college was also named by the UK *Sunday Times* as one of the 100 best companies to work for – the only FE college to have achieved such startlingly successful recognition. David's unusual wealth and depth of experience in creating outstandingly successful further education provision illuminates this unique survival guide for college leaders. David takes us from the very first principles of senior leadership – the reasons why people want to be leaders, the attributes required, preparatory steps – through every stage of taking on the job of senior leadership in a college. From dealing with your first day as a college leader, setting a mission and vision, consulting on values, strategic aims and objectives, communicating with staff and managing resources – it is all there: everything you need to know to help you take on the job of senior leadership and to become a 'difference maker'.

David expertly provides details on preparing for leadership, 'entering the fray', shaping the organization, communicating the vision, planning and resources provision, expert methods of dealing with people, performance and quality. He rounds off the book with some vivid descriptions of ways in which you can change the culture of a whole organization. David includes a range of original cartoons illustrating his text, drawn by a member of his own FE college. Helpful, practical actions are suggested throughout, to enable readers apply the vision of successful leadership to the down-to-earth, difficult realities of local FE colleges.

Finally, David leaves us at the end of this unique leadership guide with references for further reading, some of which are linked to his leadership course for new FE Principals at the Centre for Excellence in Leadership (CEL). This is a superb book on leadership, and one that will inspire improvements in the lives of generations of students to come.

Dr Jill Jameson
Director of Research
School of Education and Training
University of Greenwich
j.jameson@gre.ac.uk

Introduction

To have the opportunity to be a college leader or a senior manager is both a privilege and a challenge. It is undoubtedly a privilege to play an important role in what may well be for many a life-changing experience, and it is equally a challenge to ensure that such experiences are for the better both for the organization's staff and for its students.

Many people who are reading this introduction will have in the back of their minds that at some time in the future they might take up such a position and want to prepare as thoroughly as possible for that day. Some will already be in post and will want to do their job better. This book is about what is involved in being a successful college leader and manager. Many of the skills that are required for the most senior positions are also applicable elsewhere in the organization and consequently there are lessons within it for staff at every level.

From the outset, it would be foolish to pretend that in today's world life is going to be easy for those who find themselves at or near the top of a large public organization. If you are the principal/chief executive of a college with hundreds of staff, thousands of students and a budget of several million pounds, you will be faced with challenges at least as great as those facing the leader of a large national company. Your skills and knowledge will be tested in areas as diverse as curriculum design, financial planning, estates development and human resource management. You will be required to produce strategic plans, self-assessment reports, quality improvement programmes and an increasing level of success for students in a safe and healthy environment, managed by a happy and contented staff. You will be challenged by the national government to deliver the skills needed for the economy and by your local council for those needed to develop your community.

In many cases you will be expected to provide a comprehensive curriculum from pre-entry to degree level across a wide range of subject areas, and each year you will be tasked to do so in an increasingly efficient way. As the chief accounting officer, you will be accountable to parliament for the money you spend, and as the chief executive to an independent corporation, for the way in which you do your job. Above all, you will take on the responsibility of meeting the aspirations of thousands of individuals who will see you and the college you lead as an opportunity for a better life and often as a second chance. This means that you will need to be very clear about your vision, your values, your plans, your strategic and operational processes and about the way in which you deal with the people who work with you.

If you are a leader or manager at a more junior level, the challenges are hardly less formidable. You will have staff and students to lead and to manage, plans to make and performance targets to reach in a constantly changing and some would say increasingly difficult climate. You will need to be environmentally aware, financially acute and knowledgeable about the curriculum. You will, at various times, need to be a sociologist, psychologist, economist and a politician. You will have to balance the pressures from those above you in the organization with those who work for you. When things are going well, you will feel on top of the world as you see the positive differences that you are making to other people's lives. When times are not so good, you may feel you can hardly keep your head above water and are in danger of drowning.

At whatever level, however, there is no doubt that a college leadership and management position can be a wonderful way to spend a working life. No two days are the same and rewards can be found not only in monetary terms, but in the effects that the holder of such a post can have in developing individuals and communities towards achieving their potential.

A Survival Guide for College Managers and Leaders is a distillation of the key skills and attitudes that you will need to possess if you are to survive and indeed thrive in such a situation. It highlights examples of good, bad and questionable practice from college managers and leaders of all ages. It is a handbook of practical advice and tried and tested approaches to the many problems and challenges that you are likely to face.

From deciding that this is the role for you, through the first days in post to a consideration of the key elements of the job, you will find ideas and suggestions not only to make your life easier, but also to ensure that you are successful at what you do. In the end, you may feel that what is being described is little more than common sense, although as my grandmother used to say 'Common sense isn't so common'. Hopefully, whatever your present position, when you have read it, you will feel more confident as a leader and manager in the further education world and be ready to play a fuller part.

1 Preparing to lead

The job

No college is an island – yet in many cases they act as if they were – areas of splendid (or in some cases not so splendid) educational isolation in a choppy sea of ever-changing government policies and occasionally shark-like competitors. The better institutions recognize that they are part of a much wider archipelago, acting collaboratively with their neighbours to use their combined resources efficiently for the good of the community. They provide high-quality academic and vocational education and training programmes that meet demand, are financially secure and move forward in a spirit of continuous development and improvement. The institutions that are not so good work in isolation, performing poorly in a number of areas and often scrapping competitively for survival. Thankfully, in the England of 2006 there are very few left in this latter category, but there remains a considerable range of performance levels across the sector, as evidenced each year in the inspectorate's annual report. In most cases, this is linked to the quality of the leadership and management that the college possesses.

This variation is perhaps understandable, considering the different ways in which the government has expected colleges to operate since they were given their independence in 1993 and set adrift from local authority control. The spirit of the time was enterprise and the development of a free-market education economy. Colleges were expected to act like businesses. For some, this meant seizing every opportunity to make money – sometimes on a global basis – and a small number hit the headlines for being more active in China and in Africa than in their own backyard.

Today, the message from the government has changed. The expected course of action is now one of collaboration – the task to work with others for the common good. Yet a competitive element still remains, with each institution having to hit their Learning and Skills Council (LSC) targets and facing financial penalty or possibly even closure if they do not. For a new college leader or manager, it's a difficult balance to get right. In the world of cut-throat competition, life was relatively straightforward. Essentially, it was the survival and prospering of the fittest. Now, there is a balance to be struck between individual success and collaborative achievement. It is not always easy, for example, to work closely with schools on the one hand to deliver a vocational curriculum for the 14–16 age group, while offering an alternative and even competitive programme for those same students when they become 16. To be a successful college leader and manager in today's world, you will need to be able to resolve these conflicts.

Whatever the environment, however, the job description sent out with any application pack for the post of a college principal/chief executive is likely to have four main components. Above all, the person at the top will be expected to support the corporation in their role of determining the educational character and mission of the college, prepare the organization's strategic plan for approval, report back regularly on the college's progress and be responsible for all aspects of the day-to-day running of the institution within guidelines predetermined by the board. In particular, these will include a framework for the pay and conditions of service of staff and a set of financial regulations.

Details of what the college does and how it does it, including the appointment, grading, appraisal and, if necessary, dismissal of staff, the range and nature of activities on offer, the recruitment and support of students and the necessary activities to ensure their success, are the domain of the principal/chief executive. So too is the responsibility for ensuring that funds are properly spent and that the organization is efficiently and effectively managed.

In turn, as power and responsibility are delegated to senior managers, the way in which some of these issues will be approached will form the backbone of their job description – a mixture of leadership on key aspects of the college's operations and management to ensure that these same aspects are appropriately delivered. Together the college chief executive and senior managers will form a leadership and management team, advising the board and delivering the corporation's agreed strategy.

Leaders and followers

A search on Amazon.com for books on leadership will presently reveal over 18,000 titles on the subject, almost all of which have a particular slant on the nature of leadership and its manifestation in public and private organizations. From autocratic through creative to transformational and visionary, there is a model of leadership for almost every letter of the alphabet and often a number of important steps (ranging from three to fifty) which it is suggested will enable the reader to improve their performance. To read them all would take approximately twenty years.

As a newly appointed leader or manager with such an overwhelming choice of reading, and a demanding job, you may be best starting with a clean sheet of paper and giving some thought to two basic questions. What you would like to see in the people you lead, and what do you feel they might expect to see in you as a person to follow?

You may want to begin by considering why anyone would want to follow you and start to answer that question by looking at successful leaders of the past that you either know or have worked with. Ask yourself 'What did they have in common? What were their perceived strengths and weaknesses?' and, above all, 'Why did they succeed?'

It will be surprising if you do not find that they shared a number of key characteristics. In all probability they had a vision – a clear focus on where the organization was going. No doubt they had the ability to communicate not only that vision, but also to inspire the confidence that it could be achieved, sometimes against difficult odds. They were somehow able to channel the diverse energies of those being led towards that common goal, motivating their staff with an appropriate delegation of power and responsibility and, where necessary, support. They were possibly obsessive about achieving results. In the best of cases, they had a manner that demonstrated a set of common values that held the organization together and maintained a collective ethos. They created and maintained a culture.

Secondly, you may want to look at the characteristics of the good followers that you have encountered, without whom it would be impossible for any leader to succeed. In all probability, they in turn will have had a total commitment to the organization and its goals, and a clear recognition of the valuable and important role that they could play in their achievement. They will have been team players, but players with individual, possibly unique, skills who were positive about change and actively pursued excellence. Whatever their position in the organization, they will have taken responsibility for their own performance and its improvement.

Moreover you may well conclude that what is really important in the successful organization is the relationship between leaders and their followers. If the organization has one direction and one goal, with everyone playing their part in its achievement, then it is likely to be moving forward and developing. Both leaders and followers need to be working in harmony if lasting success is to be achieved.

What's more, if you are the chosen leader, you will realize that it's your job to make this happen. This does not mean that you have to lead the whole organization on every front and during your every waking moment. Indeed, if there is the recognition by you and others that leadership can be shared and as such can reside in a number of individuals, you are probably even more likely to be successful. This will mean that there will be times when it will be better for you to take a back seat on issues where someone else has the better skills and experience to take the organization forward. If you are able to do this comfortably, you have one of the key characteristics for a leadership position – the ability to know when to act and when to leave the action to others.

Figure 1 You simply don't seem to have a thick enough skin for the job, Mr Robinson

Where do you fit in?

Of course you may not have reached the top (as yet!) and are taking up a leadership or management role at some other level in the organization. Whatever the degree of leadership or management in your role, however, the same basic rules apply. What might not be so clear at first glance is where your part of the operation fits in to the overall picture. Are you aware of what is really expected of your function or department? Do you know how you are meant to relate to other parts of the organization? What will constitute the success or, heaven forbid, failure of your part of the organization? Sections are generally microcosms of the larger organism and as such the same rules of nature will usually apply. Hence it will be as important for you to have a clear vision and to be able to motivate and communicate to your small number of staff what is expected of them as it will be for the person at the top to lead the six hundred. If you can do this successfully, even on a relatively small scale, you are more likely to do well at the next level.

Have you got what it takes?

A useful exercise when considering a move into a leadership or managerial position is to list what you consider to be the ideal attributes of the perfect role model for that post. Be as specific as you can and aim for no more than a dozen. Next score yourself honestly out of ten for each of these and, beside each, write down the aspects of your work which you feel are strong in displaying that characteristic. Less than a 50 per cent score and maybe you're not quite ready to move on, but the chances are you will see yourself performing somewhat beyond this baseline 'pass mark'. Now comes the difficult bit. Think long and hard about what you need to do in actions and words for each attribute to move yourself towards that 'perfect ten'. Once again record your thoughts in a list. You now have a personal action plan for the way in which you are going to operate once appointed. Keep it safe and, once in post, mark yourself against it on a monthly basis. Be totally frank and honest. Wherever you are in the organization, you are really the best person to determine whether or not you are as good as you can be or what you need to do to improve.

From application to first day

So you've seen a leadership or management job that interests you, you've talked to people in similar roles elsewhere, you have thought seriously about your skills and how well they are suited to the post and now it's the time to apply. Even at this early stage, there are a number of points you need to bear in mind that will affect your performance once you are in the job. From your first contact with your potential new 'home' to that first day in post, whether you're aware of it or not, you are setting out your stall.

   Take, for example, your first telephone call or email to ask for information. Did you create the impression that you would have liked to have created? It's important to consider this, because someone will remember what you said and how you sounded and the building of your reputation will have begun. How carefully have you thought about your application? If you were sitting on the other side of the fence would you be impressed? Does it address what the selection panel are looking for? Can you match your skills to the person specification? Is the spelling and grammar 100 per cent accurate? Have you made claims or promises that may come back to haunt you?

As a general guideline, every contact you make with an organization before you are appointed should be made as if you already had the job. Not of course in an overconfident or arrogant way, but by considering the future consequences of your present actions. The people you speak to in the college should be treated as your colleagues – not members of the opposition. Be brusque with the receptionist when you turn up for your interview and you will suffer the consequences sometime later when you are in post. If it's a senior position that you are after, all eyes are going to be on you from the moment you walk in and if you really want the job you will be equally vigilant in looking for clues as to what is needed and why you are the ideal person to provide it. You then have the task of convincing the selection panel that you are the person they want.

Selection processes of course vary, but let's assume that you've had a successful interview and have just been offered the post. Whatever else you do, accept it with enthusiasm. If you're still in the college, thank all those whom you've come into contact with during the process. Be sensitive to the feelings of internal candidates and put bridge-building discussions with them high on your 'to do' list to tackle in the next few days. If you leave it any later, you may find a small army lined up against you when you arrive. Any college leadership or management job is going to be hard enough without making enemies before you start.

Remember, too, that when offered the job, it is not the time to say 'I'll think about it overnight', or 'I need to discuss it with my husband/wife/partner'. Any issues behind those statements should have been resolved long before the interview process has begun. It shows indecisiveness and uncertainty – not good characteristics to display in a leadership or management position. Ask yourself, what will your new colleagues be saying about you the next day? If it's 'They were great. They even took the time to thank me for my help', or 'They seemed to be delighted that they'd got the job', then you're off to a flying start. If it's 'I'm not sure they'll be coming. They've asked for time to think it over', what sort of impression do you think you will have made?

Deciding on an operational approach

Assuming that you've been offered the appointment, you now have some valuable thinking time as you work through the notice period in your existing post. Assuming that you want to hit the ground running, this is the time for preparation − starting with reading key documents such as the strategic plan, financial accounts, structure charts and self-assessment report, listening to the people with whom you will be working and if possible visiting your new environment. Not once − but as often as possible. You shouldn't, of course, try to make any decisions. It's not your job to do so as yet. But make notes, think about options, assess what you think needs to be done and above all consider how you are going to approach the task. Why not invite your senior team, for example, to write to you with their personal assessment of the college's or section's present performance and what needs to be done to move the organization or department forward? Not only will you pick up a number of clues as to how the organization operates, but before you have even arrived you will have already demon-strated your willingness to listen and your desire to involve others in the leadership and management process.

This is also the time to think through what sort of leader or manager you want to be and, more importantly, what you are going to do to ensure that people perceive you in the way that you would like to be perceived. What lessons have you learnt from the people you have worked for in the past? What did you like or, more importantly, not like? Which characteristics/ processes/ways of working would you most like to imitate? What would you be best to avoid? Admittedly, all this may change with time and experience, but it's not a good idea to start casually with 'We'll see how it goes'. You'll find that you will be far too busy in the early days to think about such matters. Most importantly, give particular attention to how you are going to spend your first day and your first week with your new colleagues. Now that you have the luxury of clear thinking time without the need to act, use it wisely.

Creating an image

In the immortal words of Robbie Burns, 'O wad some Power the giftie gie us To see oursels as ithers see us!' or, loosely translated, 'God give us the gift to see ourselves as others see us!' It's a gift that to the best of my experience hasn't been widely distributed. It does, however, give us a useful starting point in creating an image. Quite simply, ask yourself how do you *want* to be seen?

It's obviously your image and your decision, but at least give the matter some consideration and then, more importantly, think about what you are going to do to ensure that people see you in the best possible light. If you want to be regarded as being well organized, for example (possibly a sign of being in control or possibly of not having enough to do!), you might want to make sure that your office is de-cluttered and that your desk isn't covered with mounds of paper when people walk in. It also helps to be punctual and to deliver papers to the board in good time. Make another list: what you want to be known for and how your actions will ensure that this is the case. Then all you have to do is carry them out!

2 Entering the fray

The first days and weeks

It's your first day. The preparation is now over and you're in charge. What's more, all eyes will be on you. Anyone you meet or talk to will be asked 'What's he/she like?' So be warned. You're on!

By now, you should have spent some time 'in rehearsal' deciding how you're going to interpret the role and meeting your fellow players, but regardless of the thoroughness of your preparations there's nothing quite like 'going live'.

Start with the basics. If classes begin at 9 am, be there at 7.30 am. The British tend to respect leaders and managers who can get up in the morning and be at their desk well before other staff arrive. Although you will want to establish a positive image as soon as possible, your initial target is not to attract negative comments – 'They didn't get in until gone nine – said something about the traffic' – 'They were late for the meeting'.

You are the new leader or manager, the person in whom many will feel that their future rests. As far as the staff are concerned, you're an unknown quantity, but one that they want and need to succeed. As soon as you can, build their confidence that you can do the job. They know that their mortgage is in your hands and the sooner they feel safe and secure the sooner the organization will be able to move forward.

The people you are going to lead are also an unknown quantity to you. Be careful. There's never a second chance to make a first impression but, then again, first impressions can be mistaken. Consider carefully. Who can you trust? Who is hoping for a promotion? Where are the long-standing friendships and alliances? All of this will become clear in a relatively short period of time, but in the early days you can never be completely sure as to who or what you are dealing with. Whatever you know about college leadership and management, you will know nothing about the informal networks that exist locally and how they affect the running of the organization. The advice I was given when I started was never to speak ill of anybody or criticize anyone other than face-to-face in a one-to-one situation – and then only if there is no real alternative.

If you are the person at the top, plan an 'out and about' day in the college early in the first week so that you come into contact with as many staff and students as possible. 'We never see the boss' or, worse still, 'Who's the boss?', even if not strictly true, are complaints or comments that you have to work at preventing from the outset if you don't want them to apply to you.

Even though no two days are the same, decide what your basic routine is going to be. When are you going to deal with the post? When can telephone calls be put straight through? How are you going to handle your diary? And of course how does this fit in with those around you and their needs and preferences?

Check that you have the right equipment for the job and that you are able to tap in straight away to the communications network. Make sure that you are 'inducted', especially for health and safety reasons, both as a new employee and into your specific role. For some reason, the induction of staff in senior positions is often overlooked. From now on, though, if anything goes wrong it's likely to be your head that's on the block. You need to know what you need to know! Never be afraid to ask for advice and remember that there are experienced colleagues both internally and externally throughout the sector who will be more than willing to act as a mentor or a sounding board for the more difficult issues and problems that you may face. No one can be expected to know everything or to do the job perfectly from day one.

And finally, finish late! Even though you will find that early mornings and late nights are not necessary to do the job, they are probably necessary in the very beginning, and occasionally and randomly thereafter to demonstrate your commitment to the organization. On the one hand, you don't want to create the impression that you are struggling to cope with your workload, but, on the other, it's a good idea to demonstrate visibly that you are working at least as hard as anyone else.

When to listen and when to speak

I remember being at a conference recently when a highly successful businesswoman relayed a piece of advice that her father had given her when young: 'You have two ears and one mouth – use them in that proportion'. It's difficult to improve on advice such as that, but be careful on both counts – listening can be interpreted as silent assent and regularly talking without something interesting and relevant to say often means that those who know you will eventually stop listening altogether.

Dealing with history

For some peculiar reason, when someone starts a new job, regardless of how much experience they have had, some people will act as if the selection panel has just appointed a complete novice. Similarly, some new managers approach their first meetings with their staff as if they are dealing with people who are new to the sector rather than most likely individuals and groups with a wealth of experience between them. Try and enter the new role as if you and your colleagues are old friends who have been working together for years. Aim to bring out as early as possible evidence of their skills and experience in what you ask them to do and be quick to recognize their contribution. Your first major task is to create a new team ethos of which you are a part, not to demonstrate your own personal skills, no matter how great they may be.

It's perhaps a natural instinct for a newly appointed leader to show that they are 'in charge' and that the best way of proving that is to introduce some major changes from the outset. This can be dangerous and is often a big mistake, even if there appears to be a major problem that needs to be dealt with.

Whatever the situation, it is worth spending some time trying to get to the root cause of the issue and using the experiences of those present to help find a solution. Don't be afraid to ask very simple questions to draw out the real cause. It's amazing how often, just by having those questions answered, a solution will emerge and one that is quite different from the one that your first reactions may have suggested.

Even more difficult perhaps is breaking into new relationships. If you are the newly appointed principal/chief executive, for example, you may want to consider an early survey of how the members of the corporation feel about their knowledge and involvement and how they worked with your predecessor. If you are very brave, you might also want to think about a staff survey of how well they think the college is operating, but be prepared if you do to pick up a long list of grievances and possibly a can of worms that others will expect you to deal with. Asking people's views on specific issues carries with it an expectation that you will address them and with some sense of urgency. You might be better waiting until you have some idea of what the responses might be.

You may be lucky, of course, and be taking over from someone who has been blatantly incompetent or distant – in which case even simple positive actions may propel you towards sainthood – but this is not likely to be the case. Whatever the history, and however senior or junior your management role, it is worth taking time to find out how things used to work and initially, at least, to ensure that you only depart from these tried and tested paths for well thought through reasons. Over time, you may well want to introduce changes, but it's probably best to save your early interventions for areas where it really matters and where, if possible, everyone can see that the new is better than the old. Although change is inevitable and part of life, it does need to be paced, and change for change's sake, or merely to demonstrate that you've arrived, isn't usually a good way to start.

Time management

It probably goes without saying that the most precious commodity anyone has is time. It's a commodity that has its own rules and, contrary to popular belief, can neither be saved nor wasted. It can, however, be spent in a variety of ways and as a leader or manager you have more choice than most in how you spend that time in your working life. What is important is that, as far as possible, as a leader and manager *you* decide how your time is to be spent – not others.

Hence phrases such as 'I haven't got the time for X' or 'I'm too busy for X' should in reality be translated as 'I don't really want to do X' or 'I prefer doing Y to X'. Time isn't about saving, wasting, having too much or too little. It's about choosing what you do from a series of possibilities and deciding how much of your life you are prepared to spend doing it.

But let's start with the bigger picture. Is your aim to spend every waking moment working? Do you believe that the more hours you put in as a leader or manager the better the results? Do you feel you have to be busy to be seen to be doing the right thing? Or would you like to have a life?

I would hope that the answers are obvious. Before you begin a new job, therefore, plan your holidays. How many are you entitled to and when are you going to take them? Take your diary and mark them in before doing anything else. If you can't decide, take a possible block of time and assign it to 'Provisional holiday dates'. If you start to feel guilty, worry. You've got a problem.

Secondly, look in the mirror and repeat to yourself 'I will not take work home and I will not work on more than five days a week.' Try and keep to these rules. For many this can be really difficult, but believe me they are important if you wish to have a family and/or social life. Being a workaholic isn't something to be proud of. It's as dangerous and life-threatening as being an alcoholic. If you can't go a day without work and you're at your desk from dawn until dusk, make sure you have really good health and life insurance. They will be necessary. Stick rigidly to these two basic rules and you will not only live longer and enjoy your life more but also, surprisingly perhaps, you'll be far more effective in your job.

Thirdly, know your own body clock and when you do things best. Most people have good times and not so good times in their daily cycle. You may well find that in the morning, say from 8 am until 11 am, you are at your best. After lunch, there may be a bit of a lull and you may start to come alive again in the evening. In these circumstances, when should you schedule your most important work tasks? When should you write the strategic plan, consider the self-assessment report, draw up the budget for next year? And when do you leave time for yourself – dealing with emails, opening the post and being largely uninterrupted? There are no prizes for guessing.

It's important, too, as part of your particularly productive time periods, to allow time for thinking. For a leader and manager, thinking is work – hard work – and it should be possible to do it in the office as well as in the bathroom. Remember, if you are the person at the top, your prime responsibility is to ensure that the organization is running efficiently and effectively. That doesn't mean that you have to do everything personally. It is your job, however, to make sure that everything that is important to its success gets done. You can't do that without allowing yourself some time for reflection.

As I've already indicated, no two days are the same in this business, but a good tip is to block your productive time as relatively free (i.e. you will control what you do in it) and allocate your less productive time to activities which need to be done but which are less important to the institution and your role in it. These activities might involve meetings with other parties about their agendas, for example, awards events, or largely social activities such as presentations. When looking at your diary over a week, always leave at least one half day appointment and meeting time free to allow for the unexpected.

Colleges as they exist today also have annual cycles, almost like seasons, that relate to planning, budgeting, marketing and producing a summary assessment of performance. Work out early in your tenure when you are going to turn your attention to these issues and decide on how much time you are going to spend on each. Make sure, as well, that everyone else is aware of these cycles, so that their work is integrated into the process and planning can proceed harmoniously. At all levels, it's vitally important to be able to distinguish between what is really important, when, and then, hopefully, to allocate your time accordingly. It's no good spending so much time dealing with minor issues that you are forced to rush something that could affect the very future of the college.

Now we come to the difficult part. Deciding how much time to spend on what and learning when to say 'No'. Let's start with the bane of most organizations – meetings. These, as I'm sure you are aware by now, are great time fillers and give the illusion that everyone is busy doing something useful. Indeed I know a number of senior staff who are 'meeting addicts' – usually undiagnosed until it is too late, but essentially a condition suffered by those who feel they haven't really done any work unless they have got their daily 'fix'.

There are several ways in which you can avoid falling into this trap yourself. Firstly, by limiting the number of meetings you call to, say, three a week (an arbitrary number but what is the least number that you need?). Secondly, by limiting the notes of any meeting to date, time and duration, who was there and what was decided or what changed as a result of the meeting (i.e. no padding!). This should provide a justification for the meeting and, if it doesn't, there was probably no point in having the meeting in the first place.

Thirdly, if you want to be really hard on yourself, add up the salaries for the time of the meeting of all those present, double it for preparation time and time getting to and from the meeting, and put the cost at the bottom. This can be as effective a cure as the hair of the dog after a long night's drinking. Be brave and limit your meetings to no more than one hour. Any longer than that and everyone is likely to get bored, including you.

Then of course there are the meetings called by other people. In this case, you have to be much tougher. Your thinking should be to turn the meeting down unless you can positively see a reason why you should be there and how you are likely to make a contribution. If you're not sure, ring up and ask what

Figure 2 There are no meetings in my diary today. What on earth am I going to do?

the purpose of the meeting is and what the desired outcome might be. Remember that going to the meeting means that you have chosen to spend your time (and in essence the college's money) in that way rather than by doing something else that would possibly be more productive.

Once you are there, of course, especially if you are not the chairperson, you will have to work hard to keep the duration down to an hour. Assuming there is an agenda and any other business (AOB) is determined at the beginning of the event (good practice) you should be able to work out how long needs to be spent on each item and use your interventions to keep within the timeframe. It's a skilled game, but one that is well worth practising.

Up until now, we've largely considered organized time, but to be a successful leader you need to allow for some 'unorganized' time that can be made available to others. These are the occasions when you can respond to the 'I need to see you urgently', or 'Can I pop across?' and demonstrate your open-door policy. Scheduling these opportunities towards the end of each working day can be particularly useful. By so doing you will not only find that everyone will want to deal with the matter effectively, but they will also want to do so as quickly as possible.

Last but not least, don't spend all your time in your office. Plan walkabouts (put them in the diary) at least once a week to meet and listen to staff and students and aim to spend some of your time outside the college, in another college perhaps, or in some other part of the non-educational world. Be careful with the amount of time you are away, however. There is a little talked about 'in/out' disaster index in the sector. The more time you are away from the college above a certain threshold (usually calculated as around 20 per cent of the working week), the more likely you are to find problems back at the college when you return. There are some very famous principals who have found this out to their cost. If you want to reach a natural retirement age, this is worth bearing in mind.

In the end, of course, it's down to you to decide whether what you are doing is the best use of your time or should/could you be doing something else. Don't just ask yourself that question once though. Ask it regularly.

Space management

Although everyone is very aware that environment affects behaviour, a tour of the average college in the UK would suggest that less thought has gone into the use and presentation of space than perhaps any other aspect of college management. It's not just that space utilization factors often leave a lot to be desired, but the buildings themselves, unless they are new, are rarely presented in their best possible light.

It's difficult to work out why this is the case, especially given the number of makeover programmes on the television. After all, staff and students will probably spend more waking time in college than they will at home during the working week. Frequently, money isn't the problem either, although it invariably gets the blame. In many cases it comes down to organization and ownership.

Before looking at these two areas in some detail, college leaders and managers should be asking themselves what do students and staff want, need and expect from their college environment and how do they ensure that it is provided. First and foremost, it needs to be safe and healthy. If it isn't, the person at the top could be looking at a jail sentence. That being the case, how many new leaders and managers arrange for a full health and safety audit on appointment, as compared to those who ask for an audit of finances or student numbers?

Assuming that any obvious health and safety issues have been addressed, there then arises the question as to what systems and procedures are in place to check that standards are going to be maintained. Generally speaking, colleges are not considered to be dangerous environments, but the volume of bodies passing through institutional spaces every day, and the variety of activities in which they are engaged, means that accidents will happen. Has everything possible been done to minimize these risks and is everyone aware that health and safety comes first?

Secondly, there is a more fundamental question as to what needs to be provided and in what quantity to meet the needs, wants and expectations of those attending – all of which are rising in today's demanding world. Teaching rooms and learning spaces are the obvious starting point. Are they fit for purpose, of the right size and well appointed with appropriate equipment and technology? Are there as few of them as possible? Yes, as *few* of them as possible! Quite simply, is it better to have 100 classrooms poorly furnished and half-used or 50 classrooms fully utilized and well equipped? The costs are probably about the same.

Then there are libraries, e-learning zones and resource centres. Where are these facilities located? Are they accessible? Are they sufficient, given an increasing role for technology and self-learning? Can they be improved? Or what about the facilities that support the learner – the social spaces, eating areas, careers and counselling rooms? Or the areas that are available for staff? Do the latter, for example, have a basic 'entitlement' to space and equipment or somewhere to relax away from their students and preferably out of telephone contact? The provision of college accommodation is about meeting these needs and expectations. In that respect, it's probably more aligned to marketing than any other function. So here are a few basic suggestions.

As far as ordinary classrooms are concerned, work towards standard furniture where possible. Chairs, for example, walk from room to room when no one is looking. If they are all of the same colour and design, this probably doesn't matter too much. If they are not, then at least once a month, reorganize the stock to make each area look as good as possible. Have a basic classroom specification, which will apply to all rooms. Employ a painter to treat the college as the Forth Road Bridge and constantly paint rooms and corridors on an organized cycle. Make the public areas and corridors attractive by using professional pictures of students doing things or by displaying framed student art work.

Don't underestimate the importance of social space for people to relax and chat, especially for younger students, whose whole reason for choosing college in the first place is likely to be because their friends are going there. Buy carpet, if you still have areas of bare floors, and watch its effect on behaviour, especially where the surface changes. Running students entering a carpeted building will almost invariably slow to a fast walk. The thicker the carpet in a room, the lower the decibel level per student is likely to be.

Above all, give ownership of areas to staff and students, but at the same time give them the corresponding responsibilities to look after the area and maintain standards, e.g. 'The good news, John, is that room 201 is yours to timetable for your classes first. The bad news is that you are expected to keep it in a professional manner, with appropriate displays of materials and ensure that any maintenance issues are dealt with. You are also expected to keep it full of students!'

Then, of course, there are key management questions. Where is your office going to be – and why? Is it to be tucked away behind a Berlin wall of support staff in a no-go area (quiet so you can do some work) or in the heart of the institution (noisier, but everyone knows where you are and you know what's going on)? Where will the senior managers be located? Will they be grouped together or distributed throughout the building(s)?

There are no 'right' answers, of course, but the leader should be aware of the pros and cons of each option and make a positive decision as to why course A is being followed rather than course B. It will be an important influence on the culture of the institution. I know of one college, for example, which was not doing very well and where the senior management team (SMT) were closeted away at the end of an administrative corridor referred to as 'the corridor of shame'. If you believe that the running of a college is a team effort, the positions of the captain and other key players might just be important in determining the effectiveness of the way in which the game is played. The last thing you want to create is an 'us and them' environment.

Last but not least, there is the question of 'in-room' design. This applies to all rooms whatever their purpose but, as far as you are concerned, especially to your office or working area. Do you realize the messages that your organization of your space gives out? Personally I always make sure my office is tidy at the end of each day and before meeting anyone in it. Is your desk a barrier by its location? Can staff/students get too comfortable too quickly and hence spend more time than is necessary with you?

In my case my office has three 'zones'. I work from behind a desk facing an open door but with no chair in front of it. Hence a quick question will be dealt with by my staying where I am. Since the visitor has no where to sit down, the interchange is likely to be brief, although of course it can still be friendly and polite. There is also a meetings table in the room, surrounded by half a dozen chairs. I normally take the seat facing the clock on the wall so that I can monitor the time. Finally, there is a more comfortable area of easy chairs and a coffee table for more difficult one-to-one situations or when I do need to talk at some length. This arrangement may not suit you, but whatever you decide, do so for a reason and think about the effect on the people who will be coming to see you.

Activity management

So what exactly does a college leader do? I wish I had a pound
or dollar for every time someone has asked me that question
(usually a student on a project set by a new lecturer) and I still
haven't got a good answer. I've now resorted to saying 'I'm a
difference maker. Usually I make a difference' and hope that
they will understand why it is so difficult to summarize such a
complex series of roles. If they pursue the matter and ask 'Make
a difference to what?' I usually suggest 'To the way in which
the place operates'. More often than not, they look somewhat
perplexed and I give them a copy of my job description to put
in their portfolio.

It's a particularly difficult question to answer because, in
some ways the most important part of the job of the person at
the top is not to do anything in particular, but to see that
everything that needs to be done is being done. It is to increase
value, to make a difference, to add that something that ensures
that the organization is more successful than it otherwise might
have been. That means having a very clear idea of where the
organization is and where it is going. In turn, this requires
excellent listening mechanisms to pick up what is happening
both inside and outside the organization. It also means having
an awareness of what should be happening in the best of all
possible college worlds and a strategy as to how to get there
from where you are now. The same principles apply to a
department or a functional area. On a purely practical note,
unfortunately, none of this tells you what you should be doing
first thing on a Monday morning.

There are, however, a number of lessons from experience
that you may want to ponder over that first cup of coffee. First
and foremost is the issue of communication. In a large organization, how do you make sure that you know what's happening and that people are doing what you really want them to
do? Experience suggests that not enough time is spent in
working this through. Communication is often accidental or
very good with and between some parts of an organization (for
example the chief executive and the SMT) and very poor with
other parts (perhaps with centre organizers on campuses at a

distance). For a college to work well there has to be a clear and comprehensive communication strategy that is *designed* to hold the organization together as a whole with a common purpose. It won't happen by chance.

A good starting point is to establish a common knowledge store – a comprehensive intranet where every bit of college 'paper' is filed and accessible, including Strategic Plans, Financial Forecasts, Policies, Procedures, Minutes of Meetings and Schemes of Work. If it's not covered by the *Data Protection Act*, make it available and let everyone see whatever they want to see.

For some reason many leaders and managers find this difficult and completely innocuous documents are guarded as if they were covered by the *Official Secrets Act* or were being monitored by MI5. Ask yourself, how many papers in your college really have to be confidential and what messages does having such documents made inaccessible send to the rest of the organization? As a general rule, publish everything. Most people will never trawl through the myriad documents available to them. Some will hardly look at any of them unless they are of obvious and immediate value. All, however, will be comforted to know that they can look, if they want to, easily, and without fuss, and that there really is nothing to hide. Unless it's personal data, the word 'confidential' should never be used on anything internal without some real heart-searching as to why this is the best way to deal with the matter. Even then it's probably unnecessary.

Having an electronic filing system also saves a considerable amount of time. Ideas and materials mentioned in schemes of work, for example, can more easily be shared if they are centrally stored on the intranet, with the aim of spreading best practice throughout the institution. The latest, up-to-date version of policy X can also always be the one on the system (it's not unusual otherwise for individuals to be working from completely different versions which have been filed with varying degrees of accuracy over time).

Colleges are primarily social organizations, however, based on relationships and all relationships need to be maintained and managed. Emails, no matter how useful, are no substitute in this regard for personal contact and most colleges would benefit if leaders and managers at all levels were around and about more. Remember, though, that even on the most casual visit, especially when you are newly appointed, what you say carries great weight – so choose your words carefully and be absolutely clear as to what you mean. The person at the top casts a long shadow. Expectations can also run well ahead of what is possible – so never promise anything to anybody – ever! You can be clear about your intentions but there are so many factors outside of your control that what you may feel is a racing certainty falls at the last fence and with it your credibility.

Remember too that 'Thank yous' from those at the top of an organization are worth three 'Thank yous' from elsewhere. Don't ask me why, but they are. Even casual criticisms, if delivered by the leader, can really hurt. So it's very important that while working on your relationships from Day 1 you are careful with the messages you are sending out. Ideally, they should be reflecting the college's mission, values and aims. More importantly, you should be seen to be living these while you're on the job.

Of course you can't chat or listen to everybody. There aren't enough hours in the day. Luckily, there are multiplier effects at work here through the informal grapevine. Stop for five minutes and help a caretaker set out chairs in a classroom and probably thirty people will hear about it. Join in with the staff five-a-side football team and pretty well everyone will know. If you don't believe me, wait until you make a silly mistake and see if you don't pick up a knowing look from your newest appointee in your farthest outpost within a fortnight.

Be clear about your priorities, their importance and the time you are going to dedicate to each. Concentrate on the bigger picture for a fair bit of your time and try to make good policies and have good procedures so that you are not being constantly asked to make decisions. In the early days of an appointment you might be flattered that everyone is asking you 'Shall we do this?' or 'Shall we do that?' Don't be. Be worried. In the more successful organizations, policies, procedures, roles, powers and responsibilities are clear. Bearing in mind your leadership role, this gives you the time to concentrate on one key issue at a time, supporting those directly responsible. You'll know when you've got your policies and procedures right. You will hardly ever be asked for a decision.

When you are faced with an important matter to rule on, remember that doing nothing or delaying making up your mind may be a very good decision in itself. I'm a great believer in 'sleeping on it' and allowing my more intelligent sub-conscience to argue over the pros and cons of what I have to consider. Almost invariably, I'm much happier and clearer the next day with what I have to do. Remember, too, to keep a sense of perspective. Ask yourself from time to time how important will this really be in the history of the universe? Hold that thought and you'll undoubtedly feel better.

One final key factor in the decision-making, activity man-agement process, will be your attitude to risk – and here I would advise caution. Remember, it's not your college or, as someone once remarked, 'The senior staff shouldn't be treating this place like their personal train set'. As a college leader and manager, you have stewardship of it or part of it for a relatively short period of time and you are expected to hand it over in a better state than it was in when you inherited it. Ask yourself when committing to a big change, what is the worst that can happen and can I and the college deal with the consequences without jeopardizing any important aspects of the operation? If the answer is no or not sure – don't do it. Too many colleges have fallen into dire straits because of actions which, if everything went to plan, would solve all their problems, but if it didn't then there would be redundancies and debts. In many cases, this has been followed by a vacancy for the person at the top.

Setting the climate

Starting as you mean to go on is important when taking up a new post. How you act or react in the early days will be noted and will set the climate for weeks, months or even years to come. This is where sticking to values and principles is so important. Don't be afraid either to show the 'real you' as soon as possible, or let everyone know about your high standards and expectations. Staff will welcome this openness and the clues it gives them as to how they should respond. Most will want to support you from the outset. This is much easier if they know what is expected of them and if your likes and dislikes are displayed from the moment you arrive.

Managing expectations

Someone once told me that the secret of happiness lies in limiting your expectations. I'm not sure if that is true, but more importantly perhaps as far as college management is concerned, a great deal of unhappiness can occur if promises are made and expectations are raised that are not met. When coming new into post it is therefore best to be conservative as to what can be achieved. This is certainly the case as far as the public face is concerned, even if in your heart of hearts you believe that there are fantastic opportunities open to the organization. Doing better than people expect is good for morale, doing worse is the reverse, regardless of the absolute levels achieved. Aim for steady progress and deliver significant moves forward and you will be a hero. Over-promise and don't quite deliver and you will create an air of disappointment.

The starting point is to be realistic as to where you are now. I have known new appointees look for problems and endeavour to portray the inherited situation as badly as possible in an attempt to set the baseline at the lowest possible level. This is a dangerous game to play and is not recommended. If you are found out, it will do nothing for your credibility. Tell it as it is and give some indication as to where you think you might (conservatively) be in a year's time. Aim to be better and let everyone know that you expect them to aim to be better as well.

Entering as a potential superman or woman, or in a recovery situation as a potential 'saviour' is not where you want to be. 'Competent human' is a good place to start and your early actions should aim to establish that as your baseline.

3 Shaping the organization

Whose organization is it anyway?

Many colleges have been in existence since the middle of the nineteenth century and there are no signs that in some shape or form they will not be present in the next. As a college leader, you are effectively a guardian of an important public asset. Remember that, despite your power and responsibility, it's not your college. The real 'owners' are the public at large and as such there is a responsibility on the college leadership that their views and needs are canvassed and met, both directly and indirectly through their 'representatives', the board of the corporation. There are of course other key stakeholders who are even more directly involved: the students, whose future prospects depend a great deal on the education and skills that they develop; their employers and the other groups within which they function; and the staff. All have a right to a say on where the organization is going and how it will operate. Your role is to bring these interests together in a meaningful and targeted way so that the college has a clear mission and purpose in its community.

Mission – What's the point?

Colleges come in all shapes and sizes – from the £50 million + megaliths in some of our urban conurbations, aiming to be all things to all men, to £5 million sixth-form colleges concentrating on a relatively small portfolio of courses based on AS and A level provision. Moreover, there's pretty well every possible combination in between. What's important for everyone, however, is that they regularly review what they are doing and why they are doing it. Every now and then what is needed is a reaffirmation of purpose, if not of faith.

In the 1990s when colleges came under the auspices of the Further Education Funding Council (FEFC 1993–2001) – primarily a *funding* body – they were judged during an inspection on the range and responsiveness of their provision. They were expected to be as comprehensive as possible, usually post-16, in a largely competitive and businesslike climate. The demise of the FEFC and the rise of the Learning and Skills Council (LSC) – a *planning and funding* body – have changed these rules.

Today colleges are meant to concentrate on what they are good at, playing a role as key providers in a collaborative environment whose overall comprehensiveness and coherence is the responsibility of the LSC. Missions can therefore be refined and colleges more focused, without the need for pangs of conscience or even guilt that not every local education and training issue is being addressed.

There has also been the emergence of a 14–19 agenda, increasing the range of operations that falls within the college's possible remit. With the average lifetime now stretching to almost 85 years, if we recognize that the need for learning new skills never stops, the work of colleges potentially covers more than 85 per cent of the population's educational needs. It's a sobering and possibly worrying thought.

So what should the college in which you work do? Most college missions are pretty well identical and could just as well have been photocopied, with the name changed to suit the college in question. What's more there probably isn't a lecturer nationally who could quote their college's mission word perfectly (usually 20 or 30 words long). A regular mission re-examination is a real opportunity to concentrate on the key strengths of the organization and steer clear of any areas that the college doesn't feel it either is or can be good at. Are you focusing on skills for employment? Is your primary focus to regenerate your local community? Are you striving for academic excellence? What is really important to you and what is less so? After all, if everyone isn't clear as to what the organization is really about, what hope is there? Try and keep the mission specific, focused and stated in as few words as possible.

Vision – Where are you going?

At the time of incorporation in 1993, Sir John Harvey Jones, the business guru of the time famous for his work in ICI and advice to struggling companies, was invited to address college leaders as to how he would set about running a college. At the end of a very useful and perceptive presentation, he was asked by one of those present what he thought of three-year strategic plans then being prepared by institutions in many cases for the first time. The great man smiled and said 'One year is a plan. More than that is a dream.'

Given the number of twists and turns of government policy since then and the regularity of new initiatives, there are few survivors of those early days in the new world who would disagree with him. That said, as sleep researchers will confirm, dreaming is important to our individual well-being. It's also important for a college to progress.

A useful exercise that a new leader can undertake is to get the staff to imagine themselves ten years down the line and a newspaper headline which states 'College/Department X has been officially recognized as the best in the country'. The task is for the staff to write the article realistically and in as much detail as possible, explaining why. This should include detailed facts and figures when student or staff performance measures are mentioned. The second part of the exercise is to hold an honest discussion as to why the college or department is not there now (which of course assumes that everyone knows where the college or department actually is now), and the third – you've guessed it – a piece on how the gap(s) might be closed. You then have the bones of a long-term plan. Incidentally ban all references to 'There's not enough money' or 'It's the students' fault'. They are hardly ever valid reasons why colleges aren't successful.

As with so many planning activities, what you will discover in the course of this exercise is that it is the process itself that brings the real benefit rather than the output. At the end of the day, if you have a general agreement as to where you are aiming to be and how you might get there, you have more than a sporting chance of turning a dream into a reality.

Values – How are you going to get there?

While most, if not all, colleges have a mission statement and many have a long-term vision as to what the organization might look like in five or ten years' time, the existence of a set of values that will determine *how* the college will operate is somewhat rarer. Yet in many ways, this is of more importance to the long-term success of the organization than the first two. A set of corporate values is not about what you do – it's about the way that you do it and, if well thought-out, provides the overarching principles on which the college's policies and procedures will be formed and its operations judged. Values should set the 'tone' of the organization and time and trouble should be taken with actual and potential employees to ensure that they are comfortable with the basic principles enshrined therein.

As a public-sector organization, the seven principles of corporate life – selflessness, integrity, objectivity, account-ability, openness, honesty and leadership – as set out by the Committee on Standards in Public Life in 1996 (Nolan Committee 1996) are a good starting point for a set of values, but there will be additional emphases that you may wish to incorporate. Equal opportunities, for example, is perhaps a stronger concern now than it was ten years ago. You may also wish to include additional elements of style or approach, e.g. 'Management should be more about guidance and support than regulation and control.' Or 'Quality is at the heart of all we do. In our pursuit of excellence we recognize that individually and collectively we can always improve.'

Both the values and their precise wording need to be thought about carefully, with widespread consultation. Most colleges who have embarked on this path, however, have generally found agreement fairly easy to achieve and the values they have come up with seem almost universal. It's perhaps reasonable therefore to start with someone else's list and ask for suggestions and modifications. It's then a case of going around a reiterative loop until there is a consensus. The result, once agreed, is a major contributor both to security (people know how they are expected to behave) and unity (everybody is behaving broadly in the same way). In an organization where there are so many different and in many cases unique jobs, this is invaluable.

Having a set of values is one thing, however, but demonstrating them in practice is another. For the college leader or manager, this is the real challenge. A useful exercise is to make two columns, listing the values in column one and the way in which you demonstrate them at work in column two. If you feel really brave add a third and list actions that may be interpreted as working in the opposite direction. I know one new principal, for example, who was very happy to recognize that everyone potentially could make an equal contribution to the success or failure of his organization and indeed of the importance of equal opportunities in the running of the college, but was much less happy when it was suggested that reserved parking places solely for senior managers could be interpreted as something quite different. It's best to practise what you preach.

Strategic aims and objectives – Steps along the way

Having established your mission, general vision and overall values, the next step is to turn these thoughts and ideas into a framework for action covering the next three to five years. This is the strategic plan. Remember that it is a *plan*, not a straitjacket. It is designed to highlight priorities and create a common focus. Structures and content will vary, but in one way or another a strategic plan will usually start with an overview of where the college is now (the starting point in terms of quantity and quality), will outline the environment in which the college will be working (competitive/collaborative), will move on to a national/regional/local needs analysis, and will then state the general contribution the college is aiming to make in meeting those needs. Usually, there will then be a section as to how progress is going to be measured and the identification of a number of interim steps along the way. Once completed, the overall responsibility for approving the plan lies with the brand, but the principal/chief executive will be expected to give professional guidance as to what is most appropriate.

Subsections of the above may include details of the programmes to be offered, how they are going to be marketed and ways in which resources will be allocated. The better plans usually conclude with a get-out clause suggesting that they are plans, not promises!

In whatever the form the strategic plan is presented, however, there needs to be a clear delivery and monitoring strategy aligned to it. In this respect, it can be useful to assign individual strategic aims to each of the members of the senior management team (SMT) as overall 'guardians' and to ensure that they report back to the corporation on a termly basis as to what has been achieved. The SMARTer the aims (specific, measurable, achievable, relevant and timely), the easier this will be, although it is often a good idea to list activities that the college is undertaking which those responsible believe are moving the college in the required direction, even if a direct effect can't really be calculated. The subsections will have objectives attached and, once again, it will be the responsibility of the SMT to ensure that they are delivered – for example, annual student full-time equivalent (FTE) numbers for the member in charge of the curriculum, and end of year bank balances for the director of finance.

Determining policies and procedures

Once the direction of the college has been set and generic ways of operating determined (the values), a well-run institution needs a series of detailed guidelines (policies and procedures) that will inform its day-to-day activities and ensure a consistent operational approach. Generally speaking, the larger and more complicated the organization, the more important these are. Summed together they make up a 'work manual', the equivalent of standing orders – a point of reference for decision-takers throughout the organization.

The more comprehensive these are, the less likelihood there is for dispute and disagreement. They range from complaints, grievance and disciplinary matters through procedures for determining the appointment and grading of staff, to the ways in which students are to be dealt with from application to departure. They can also include internal and external service-level agreements. A sign of a well-run organization is an easy availability to a comprehensive set of such documents so that anyone can refer to them as necessary. A weak organization will have less of a range, leaving a large number of issues up to the judgement of individuals. With the best will in the world, over a relatively short period of time, this will lead to inconsistencies and at the very least irritations, as individuals can see no clear reason why they have been treated in one way while others have been treated differently. At worst, there will be complaints and major disputes.

A good 'entry point' for a new leader or manager is therefore to ask for an up-to-date set of policies and procedures and see what turns up. Do they cover all major parts of the running of the organization or are there important areas missed out and therefore subject to ongoing individual judgements? Is each one clear and, as a set, are they consistent? If not, there is work to be done. The objective is not to create a series of straitjackets with every movement subject to regulation and control, but to set clear boundaries within which individuals feel secure and free to operate. Rather than continually having to ask 'What do I do about X?', individuals can refer to policies and procedures that have been thought-through and suggest solutions.

Where there are important pieces of the policies and procedures jigsaw missing or where existing guidelines seem out of date or inconsistent with the college's higher level aims and values, or indeed with each other, this is an excellent opportunity to consult and get as many views as possible as to the way forward. Starting with setting out what the present situation is and what you want to achieve in general terms offers a good framework for individuals or groups to add their contributions. Depending on the importance of the policy in question, this may be as simple as a one-off email request for suggestions to a series of discussion groups over a period of time. The desired outcome is for the issue to be fully considered and an agreed way of proceeding established to cover foreseeable circumstances.

Figure 3 Well, that's 257 decisions we've made this week between us. That must have made a difference, surely?

When to make decisions and when not to

As a general rule, it is better for a college leader to make or help make policies and procedures from which decisions flow than to make decisions. New to post, it may seem exciting to be continually asked 'Should we do this or should we do that?' It may even be taken as a sign of the importance of the leader to the organization. In fact, if the phone is always ringing and people don't know what to do, the reality is it is just the reverse.

It's a sign of weakness and is an important area to address. Remember, the aim is for all staff to be confident to take decisions in the areas for which they are responsible, having clear policies and procedures to guide them and to ensure that whatever decision they take, it doesn't move the organization off its general course.

Monitoring your performance and the performance of the organization

Determining a mission, having a vision, a strategic plan and a set of aims and objectives, backed up by a comprehensive series of policies and procedures to help achieve these are all well and good, but what everyone will want to know, sooner or later, is how well the organization is doing. It would be true to say that in many colleges the monitoring of performance is often less well done than the planning process itself, although it is essentially part and parcel of the same activity – the closing of the loop to set the baseline for the next plan.

Performance, of course, can be monitored at all levels – college, faculty or curriculum area, department, team, student group or individual. At whatever level, however, there needs to be a determination of what is/are the appropriate activities to measure, the unit of frequency of measurement and, perhaps most importantly, what you are going to do with the results when you have them. The advent of significant computer power and a national obsession with data collection and analysis means that there may well be umpteen statistics available to you for almost every aspect of the college's operations. This doesn't mean that they are all useful or relevant. Having a plethora of data at your fingertips isn't the same as having a good management information system. The trick is to know and to be able to monitor what is really important and what you can influence. A good exercise is to ask yourself what is the least number of indicators that you and the corporation need to have to assure you that the college/faculty/department is on 'track' to achieving its aims. You then need to make sure that you have this information in time to make a difference.

For each performance measure, there needs to be a confidence level with regard to its relevance and accuracy. The latter doesn't of course have to be 100 per cent. The point of a performance measure is to improve performance. Recording what is or was may only be of passing historical interest, and refining a measure to X places of decimals may be a waste of time and effort. Ask yourself, what do you need to know and how accurate does it need to be to help you run the organization? And settle for that.

Setting minimum performance standards across the college is also useful. The floor will vary from college to college and will take into account local circumstances, but there should always be a floor, and over time you should expect that floor to rise.

More controversial, however, is the setting of ceiling targets. Is there a limit as to how good you want to be? It may seem like a ridiculous question but some desired outcomes may be in conflict with others. On the one hand, you may wish to widen participation, for example by encouraging those who are less familiar with education to participate, and hence who may find it more difficult to achieve; on the other hand, you may want success rates to rise. Be clear as to the trade-offs and what are acceptable levels of compromise. Be careful too that local targets do not damage overall performance, as individuals or groups strive towards their goals without really considering the overall effect on the organization.

Comparisons against benchmarks should also be taken very seriously – particularly within the organization, comparing what is happening now with what has happened previously. Whatever the outcome – moving forwards, backwards or staying the same – there should be an equal intensity of investigation as to why the performance is different. Can the reasons for the change be determined? What degree of confidence do you have in the results? Can you decide on future actions from what you have found out?

Once again care is needed – especially in trying to link cause and effect too closely. You may think you can see a link, but rarely can you be absolutely certain. I once remember reading that the human birth rate in Sweden and the number of nesting storks seem to move in parallel. In a college you have to take care when benchmarking to check that there is real comparability of like with like and that the comparison is at a sufficiently detailed level to make sense. A high number of applications at a particular time of year as compared to last year, for example, is an encouraging sign, but may not indicate an increase in the overall total at the end of the day. People might just be applying earlier.

This doesn't mean that examining the reasons for performance, even with limitations of accuracy and certainty, is a waste of time. The process of past and present performance examination, if done well, will not only give you a better understanding of what appear to be the key component parts in determining the performance outcome, but it should also give you a clearer indication of what, on the basis of the evidence you have, you should/could do next. On the whole, though, benchmarking statistics tend to be more useful when taken in groups. Applications are up, a greater proportion of students are appearing for interview and more are accepting their offers of a place. Taken together, it would seem sensible to plan for some growth.

To improve their usefulness further, comparisons with other colleges and their performance in the same area are particularly useful. 'Twinning' with another college or group of colleges and discussing relative performance and the perceived reasons for it can be a considerable aid to quality improvement. The same of course can apply to a faculty, department or an individual.

4 Communicating the vision

Leadership and delegation

Colleges are not democracies. Neither the appointed leader nor their senior staff in the form of the management team are elected and neither are their responsibilities likely to be so devolved that they will avoid the blame if things go wrong. That doesn't mean to say that the leader should not have a range of methods at his or her disposal to find out the views of others who have a stake in the success or failure of the organization. Given the opportunities offered by the new technology, this can include an email referendum on a particular issue, a series of task groups to come up with solutions to a particular problem or soundings of ideas tried out while on walkabout.

The real issue is that, although a leader or senior manager can delegate their power, they cannot pass their responsibility down the line. The buck stops with them and the final responsibility for every aspect of the college's operations should rest firmly with a senior management team (SMT) member. Asking who's responsible for that success or that failure, one hand and one hand only should go up.

This doesn't mean of course that credit for success should not be 'delegated'. As Jim Collins suggests in *Good to Great* (Collins 2001: 35), when things go right, look out the window to find someone to credit, even if you really feel it was down to you. When they go wrong, it's probably best to look in the mirror.

Communications by design

If communications are such an important and natural part of human behaviour, why is it that 'poor communications' almost invariably figures towards the top of any poll as to where an organization is going wrong or what needs to be improved? As such, it should be one of the main issues for any leader or manager to address. The college equivalent of 'Send reinforcements, we're going to advance' morphing into 'Send three and four pence, we're going to a dance' is not uncommon. To avoid that happening to you, it is necessary to realize that good communications do not happen by accident. As I have suggested before, they happen by design.

First, the obvious – basic communication is at least a four-way process. A message is sent; a message is received. A reply is sent; a reply is received. Add in processing or interpretation at each point of reception and the complications of an organizational hierarchy and there are many points where matters can go awry. Bearing this in mind, it's maybe not quite so surprising that poor communications are common and messages don't always get through.

Secondly, the equally obvious – we communicate in a variety of ways, including words, gestures and movements but by far the most important are words. Whether written or spoken, they should be chosen carefully to ensure that the right message is at least sent. Remember too that the spoken word is rarely recorded in day-to-day business operations, but the written word can last for ever. Before you rush to respond to that annoying email, bear that in mind. Maybe it would be better to discuss the matter directly with the individual than fire off an angry (and irretrievable) reply?

In written communication, staff, students and others will be expecting high standards of grammatical correctness and spelling from their leaders and managers. If this is one of your weaknesses, make sure that it doesn't show and work on putting it right. You're leading a place of learning or a section thereof. What kind of message is being sent if communications from you are poorly written?

Where prospectuses and external communications are concerned, the expectations double. Special care will need to be taken to rule out any unintentional hidden messages. Do the pictures in your prospectus stereotype students into traditionally male or female occupations? Is there an appropriate gender/race balance? Are students with disabilities taken account of? What are the key points that you really want to get across and are they clearly made? Having a clear checklist of 'must haves' is useful. Testing the final draft product before print with students and staff can also be very illuminating and can save an expensive or even embarrassing mistake.

Thirdly, there are a variety of methods of communication, some of which are more suitable than others for particular situations. With the spread of email, not only are the skills of letter writing beginning to fall into disrepair (and there are times when a letter is much more appropriate to the circumstance) but there are some managers who are in danger of forgetting that the telephone or indeed a direct face-to-face conversation is sometimes the quickest and best way to get a message across.

Having mastered these basics, there remain the vital questions of who to communicate with, when, where and how. This assumes of course that you've sorted out the 'what' – which is not always the case. Opening the mouth before the brain is in gear is unfortunately a trait not confined to less experienced staff.

In general, it helps to structure some time into the week when essential communication activities can take place. Course delivery, for example, is usually a team activity and from time to time it will be necessary for all those involved to get together to discuss course content and progress and how the student members of the group are fairing. Left to ad hoc arrangements, and depending on the overlap or otherwise of timetables, this may or may not happen, with almost inevitably a damaging effect on quality. If you timetable communications into normal activity as a requirement, the chances are that it will take place.

There are a range of curriculum and non-curriculum activities to which this applies. Staff will need to meet to plan future activities, self-assess the progress of their area and monitor their ongoing development plans. Non-curriculum teams will need to meet to discuss system improvements. All are much more likely to be successful if there is a specific time set aside to address these issues.

The same applies to staff development. In many colleges, this is a relatively ad hoc process linked more closely to individual requests to attend courses and conferences than based on a series of planned activities to assist in the achievement of strategic objectives. Essential as all these activities are, however, the main purpose of any college is delivering a first-class education service to students and their teaching and learning activities are paramount. Timetables should not be interrupted for administrative or training purposes, no matter how important. A useful edict at the beginning of a new leadership or management regime may well be 'Teaching the students comes first'. Believe it or not, there are people who would rather attend meetings than be in the classroom.

One way of dealing with this dilemma is to set aside an amount of dedicated 'meeting and activity time' during which no teaching takes place and in which all these subsidiary but nevertheless important support activities can be held. Realistically, this is likely to amount to one half day a week, especially if some aspects of the staff development programme are included. Once identified, the variety of necessary meetings need to be timetabled in, recognizing that several discrete groups can meet at the same time, and a 'calendar' for the year drawn up, identifying, for example, when the self-assessment report will be considered, when student progress will be discussed or when internal verification will take place. As far as possible, all key activities should be included (college staff meetings and faculty meetings, for example) and published well in advance. Where there are teaching staff involved, full-time students who are to be in the college at the time are either timetabled onto enrichment activities, sport and team games or self-study. Part-time student courses are not timetabled to coincide with the half-day slot.

This planning of ongoing activities can apply equally well to what is to be discussed at various meetings throughout the year. For each board or sub-committee meeting, for example, it is possible to list at least 90 per cent of the papers and reports that will be discussed at least a year in advance. This also has the advantage of ensuring that nothing important gets forgotten. The same process can apply at academic board, faculty, department and course team level. If the minutes of these meetings are also confined to a list of those present, what has been decided and any follow-up actions allocated, then for most colleges, some important aspects of good meetings will also have been addressed.

As a leader or senior manager it is useful too if you can plan your own communication time – at least in part. If you are dealing with a multi-sited operation, make sure you allocate regular time to each campus. Walkabouts should be treated in the same way as an important meeting and allocated time in your diary. Otherwise it's too easy to put them off. They should also be targeted at different parts of the college at different times of the day/week to ensure that everywhere and ideally everyone is covered. Other good ideas which have worked elsewhere include monthly informal lunchtime meetings with representatives of various sections of the college, new starters' meetings shortly after they have taken up post to discuss what they have noticed about the way in which the college operates, and SMT focus groups with students and staff, again perhaps on a monthly basis.

There are many other ideas which could be included here – regular newsletters, weekly bulletins, log-on reminders of today's activities, consolidated 'to do' lists – and each manager will have their own favourites. The important message is to design and build the communication system that is going to take place. Don't just assume that it will happen automatically or by chance.

Data collection and interpretation

With the advent of the computer, the availability of information to the college manager has increased by more than a hundredfold, to the extent that many people are now complaining of information overload. As a leader or manager you obviously need to know how well you are doing at any point in time and there are a number of figures that can be called upon to help you. But what are the key figures, what will they tell you and how often should you be looking at them?

Let's start with some general principles. To be of any use, a management information system has to produce timely returns. If you have set a budget and have calculated what you will be spending in each category, your main concern is to be warned of any key element which is going off course (you need the equivalent of a flashing red light) and to be aware of the problem in time to do something about it.

Similarly, it's no use knowing at the end of the year that you are not going to achieve your LSC contract because your student numbers are too low. What you really want to be made aware of is anything that is deviating from plan as soon as it becomes apparent, so that you can immediately institute corrective action. In this respect, you have to be realistic. Full-time students are generally recruited by colleges at the beginning of each academic year. A fall in numbers by 1 October is not going to be corrected in that year and resources may need to be adjusted accordingly. More importantly, next year's assumptions should start with the belief that what you are seeing now is the start of a new trend and adjustments are made as necessary. Plan for the worst and be pleasantly surprised when it doesn't happen.

Secondly, you need to be wary of data interpretation. This is as much an art as a science. Take what may appear to be a simple situation. How many students do we have this year as compared to the same time last year? This may seem like an easy question to answer but are you comparing like with like and what do the raw figures actually mean? An increase in total student numbers, while apparently comforting, may tell you very little, for example, about the amount of work you are doing or about the relative income they are generating. This year, you may have done a lot more short-course work, for example, inflating the view of the progress that you think you have made. Full-time equivalent (FTE) students are a better guide, but in today's world, not all FTE students are worth the same. A significant drop in the number of engineering students (high-income producers) which is balanced by an equal rise in business studies students (average income earners) means a drop in receipts. What's more, an apparent rise in numbers at a particular time of year may be more about a greater efficiency in transferring enrolments into the main student record system than anything else.

For every key statistic, it is useful to give it a probability rating in your own mind as to how reliable it is as a decision-making tool. Don't forget that some data is likely to be important to all staff in the institution, but gathering it and having it is of no use whatsoever if staff can't interpret it and use it to inform their actions. In most colleges, this is a major staff development activity. For whatever reason, many people are not comfortable with the interpretation of figures and yet it is an essential part of so many college jobs. For a main-grade lecturer, the ability to calculate and set value-added targets for his or her students, interpret trends in performance, and read attendance statistics or graphs in a meaningful way are all important. A quick numeracy test for staff (if you had the nerve to do one) would show you how much there is to be done.

Ensuring that the right people have the right information at the right time

The best way of doing this is, as I have suggested, to start by creating a kind of 'Encyclopedia Collegia' on the staff intranet, with every piece of college information on it and a search engine to help track it down. Given the range of material, this is best kept up-to-date by allocating responsibility for small sections to individuals and by having a regular spot audit to make sure that what you think is happening is really the case.

Next comes the slightly more difficult task of determining what each member of staff needs to be keeping an eye on and with what frequency. Take a head of faculty, for example. Their list might include student numbers as compared to last year and annual targets (weekly), student attendance rates (weekly or monthly), student retention figures as compared to last year (monthly), student achievement and success rates as compared to last year (annually), staff utilization figures (termly), staff sickness figures (weekly and termly), staff turn-over (termly), income generated against target (monthly),

Figure 4 The only thing that's going up around here is the number of targets I have to achieve

consumable budget spend against allocation (monthly) and part-time teaching hours against allocation (monthly). All of these, incidentally, are also likely to be of interest to you if you are the principal/chief executive.

What you don't want, however, is staff spending a lot of time gathering this information. You need a system that will do this for them. The role of staff is in interpreting the information provided for them and instituting any necessary action to ensure that the activity under examination is going as well as possibly can be expected.

Gathering feedback

So far we've looked at ways of communicating with and gathering feedback from those within the institution. There are clearly other stakeholders, however, whose views are equally important, starting with the corporation. This is an interesting area. On the one hand, if you are the principal/chief executive, you will want your board members to know everything about the workings of the institution for which they are ultimately responsible, but, on the other hand, you will be acutely aware of their time limitations as volunteers. You are also likely to be conscious of the fact that the more they know about the day-to-day operations, the more possible it is they will want to interfere in what is really your job. This is a potentially tricky situation. On the same basis as the principle of 'letting all staff know everything they want to know' outlined above, it is a good idea to allow access to 'Encyclopedia Collegia' to corporation members. It's also a good idea to expose the corporation to staff and students, although after a clear reminder of where the dividing line between governance and management lies. A successful way of doing this is to link a board member with a curriculum or cross-college area (possibly on an annually rotating basis) and encourage them to visit that area to get an idea of how it operates. An extension of this is to encourage them to present the self-assessment report for that area to the corporation meeting where it is to be reviewed. This will ensure that they understand the strengths and weaknesses of the operation and the actions necessary to take the college forward.

The key to good communications with the board, however, is the clerk – not only in terms of the clerk ensuring that board members have timely, relevant and succinct papers and reports to consider, but also that any other matters of relevance and interest are regularly brought to their attention. A regular weekly email or written bulletin including a summary of internal matters of interest and any key national issues from the *Times Educational Supplement* (*TES*) is a feature of some colleges and one that works well. It may also help having the clerk attend each SMT meeting so that they can pick up any items that are of interest to the board and report back. They should also let board members know of college events/activities that they might like to attend and ensure they have the appropriate invitations. A good clerk is a godsend to a college and to the principal/chief executive, who otherwise may spend an inordinate amount of time keeping the board informed and happy, rather than doing the job for which they are paid.

When it comes to other stakeholders, once again a system is required, but it is perhaps less clear as to how much time and effort should be distributed in this direction. Letting others know what the college is doing and finding out what others would like it to do are both important, but as virtually the whole adult population in the area probably has some kind of interest in these matters, limiting decisions need to be taken.

Probably of greatest importance is the way in which the press, especially the local press, is handled. There will of course be advertising carried out during the year, but colleges are a good source of filling copy for local newspapers (e.g. 'Students cook up a storm to raise money for charity, etc.') and it is certainly worth considering the appointment of a press officer to look for these stories, write them in a way that the local press find useful and deliver the column inches. Here, performance can be measured in terms of column inches and the numbers and variety of stories covered. If the press are slightly less forthcoming, the advertising feature – selected stories, pictures and the odd advert – taking a page each month – can be money well spent.

Another effective way of getting messages across, although not so good for the waistline, is the use of 'events' – business breakfasts for chief executives or senior business men and women, focus group lunches for community groups, dinners perhaps for head teachers. In all cases, the question to be asked is 'What will make this an attractive activity for the target audience to attend?' A classic is the traditional presentation of the college's annual report for the year. On its own, this is hardly a top draw, although a great opportunity for the college to sell itself. If, however, you add in a first-class speaker, local or national, the meat in the sandwich, suddenly you have something much more palatable all round. As with all communications, 'listeners' are needed, as well as 'broadcasters' and there are times when you will really have to think about how you are going to attract an audience. Just make sure that whatever you come up with is good value – £ for lb.

5 Planning and marketing the programme

Assessing demand

There comes a point very early on, of course, when all college managers will need to turn their attention to the college programme. What exactly are they going to offer and how is it going to be delivered? The fairly obvious place to start is market research and in this area there is any amount of information available on general indicators of potential demand, such as employment statistics, growing and declining sectors of the economy and population trends. Unfortunately for the individual college leader and manager, these are not a great deal of use in charting the way forward.

There are several problems, for example, with relying on general indicators of demand, mostly summed up in the phrase, 'lies, damned lies and statistics'. First and foremost, there is an issue with data and what it does and does not tell you. Even if the information has been reliably gathered and the figures are statistically significant (not always the case, by any means), it is difficult to see how knowing that there is a national shortage of construction skills, for example, will help you to plan for a particular college or department.

The first problem concerns the demand side for skills. Never mind what is happening nationally, the important question is does this reflect the local situation? What skills are missing and how many people would it take to fill them? Is the area down for a major expansion of house-building or is all that is left green-belt or a number of small brownfield sites to infill? Are the firms that might be awarded contracts likely to bring in their own workforce from Eastern Europe or elsewhere? Will the desired route for training, if needed, be through full-time courses or apprenticeships? And, given the building cycle and the students you are about to train, how important is the time lag?

The second problem concerns the supply side. If the information you have received is generally available, what will the effect be if everybody else decides to jump on the construction training bandwagon? Skills needs and employment opportunities may both be rising – there may even be more training being undertaken – but *your* numbers could be in decline.

Where you're looking at changes in, for example, engineering, the problem is even more complicated. An expanding manufacturing industry may or may not mean more skilled jobs. I know of one well-known national major company that has more than tripled its output and labour force over the last four years. Their requirements for technical skills, however, were minimal. Their real requirements were for employees to have the ability to turn up on time, work hard and adapt to the new technology. If the local college had expanded its engineering training capacity in anticipation of more work it would have made a costly mistake. A robotic production line was doing most of the increased work.

In reality, the best source of labour market information is likely to be the number of students who are applying for the courses that you can provide and the trends therein. Although some individuals may take what appear to be strange decisions, the public, as a whole, tends to act logically. After all, their decisions are based on the same kind of information that you have, plus their personal experience and knowledge of what opportunities are available. Moreover, they are investing their time and money in their own training, so there is a real incentive to get it right. For many, too, their market is not a local one – it may be regional, national or international. Resist, therefore, any pressure from your local educational planning body not to offer certain training because 'there is no demand in the area'. At South Cheshire College we were once refused the opportunity to develop a travel and tourism centre of vocational excellence, despite excellent results and a high demand for courses, because Crewe 'wasn't really a tourist area'. Unfortunately, we weren't successful in getting the message across that our ex-students were being employed in tourism not only all over the UK, but all over the world, and, hard as it was to believe, not everyone wanted to stay in Crewe for the rest of their lives. By all means, have a range of networks by which you pick up the word on the street and follow up specific leads. This may reveal new opportunities, but watch and analyse your application trends carefully. They are the real basis for assessing the future demand for courses.

Deciding on what you offer and what you don't offer

The easiest way of deciding what you do and do not do is to provide what you do well and leave out anything where you cannot offer a good-quality product. Very few colleges can be efficient and effective across all curriculum areas, though many strive to be so. Remember that the adequacy and sufficiency of local provision is the responsibility of the local LSC, not you. When you are new into post this is a good time to conduct a curriculum audit. Make a list of all that your college does and the numbers of full-time, part-time and FTE students who have enrolled in each curriculum area. Have you got an appropriate range of quality courses? How good are the results? What happens to the students at the end of their programmes? Are there opportunities for progression? Can you map these opportunities and how many students are likely to follow them through?

Unfortunately, sometimes the answers to these questions will give rise to even more queries than those you had when you started. I remember a few years ago a BTEC National Diploma Course in Computing where 24 students all succeeded and all got jobs within a month of leaving college. Not one of those jobs, however, was in computing. So was the course a failure (no computing jobs) or a resounding success (transferable skills that were in heavy demand across a range of occupations)? Then there comes the really thorny issue. Are you really only concerned with what happens in the few months after the course has ended? The real results in terms of how useful a programme may have been may only surface a number of years down the line.

Figure 5 Are you sure these lap dancing courses are really being demanded by employers?

The same sort of argument can apply to pretty well all curriculum areas. Many colleges are training literally hundreds of hair and beauty students each year, yet local salons are continually advertising vacancies. The skills in customer service and attention to a smart appearance are an attraction to many other areas.

If you want my advice, it would be to concentrate on getting the quality right and not to worry too much about matching programme content precisely to perceived needs. The experience of being recognized as a successful student is what is probably most useful in the long term to both the individual and the employer. This is not a common view, but experience suggests that it works.

Producing the plan

Putting all this together should enable you to come up with a core programme for the term or year, with realistic numbers estimated, based on historical conversion rates (enquiry to interview to enrolment). Numbers do fluctuate from year to year, but normally on a trend pattern in each curriculum area. At the beginning of 2006, for example, business studies numbers seem to be on a gradual decline, while media studies numbers remain on the way up. Just occasionally there is an unexpected surge of interest when a new television series suddenly glamorizes an occupation heretofore overlooked (forensic science being a recent UK example), but generally there is a discernible pattern.

The plan then needs to be 'resourced' and there are various ways of doing this. For a number of years, I have worked with a model based on nominal average class sizes, set teaching hours for full-time provision and a basic fee rate per hour for part-time work. Other successful models include those that cost each course and expect a contribution in the region of 40 per cent to overheads (depending of course on your definition).

In summary, the class size/student hours model goes something like this:

College programme

The college programme is produced following an analysis of market information and discussions with each programme area manager. Standard 'teaching' hours are allocated to full-time courses – perhaps 576 hours a year for a student on a BTEC National programme and 180 hours for one studying an A-level subject. An additional tutorial hour is made available to each group of students to cover citizenship and other topics of general interest, and personal academic tutorial time is given on the basis of 2 hours per student per year (2 × 20 minute-meetings per term). Part-time course hours are determined by programme areas, after considering the amount of time required to deliver the programme against income. The fees charged are then based on a common agreed hourly rate.

Staff hours
Nominal class sizes are applied to each programme area, determined by the mix of practical and theoretical work. These could be as high as 16 (for highly practical subjects such as catering), 18 (for 'mixed economy' work such as art and design), or 20 (for mainly theoretical, classroom-based studies). By multiplying the allocated hours per student by the projected number of students and then dividing by the nominal class size, the number of staff teaching hours required can be calculated for each course and each programme area. This does not necessarily represent the number of guided learning hours needed to deliver each programme, since students may be allocated additional time or work in the learning resource centres (LRCs) or other study areas.

Part-time teaching hours allocation
By subtracting the sum total annual number of teaching hours agreed for each established member of staff from the total number of staff teaching hours required to run the programme, and adjusting for any 'servicing' (staff exchange) arrangements between programme areas, a part-time teaching hours allocation for each area can be determined.

FTE targets
Based on the above calculations, each programme area is set an FTE student target to be achieved with the allocated resource. Dividing the total number of student taught hours by, for example, 540 gives the number of FTEs.

Income targets
On an annual basis, each programme area is set an income target following discussions between the head of faculty and the director of finance.

Consumables
Consumables are allocated to each programme area on the basis of x pounds per FTE. These can be weighted to reflect the additional cost of practical courses. In addition, or as an alternative, all full-time students can be allocated a sum of money to

the value of £y per year to spend on books and consumables. Students may also apply to the college for additional support for books and equipment, depending on their personal circumstances.

Capital equipment

Capital equipment for each year is allocated to programme areas following a bidding process and discussions of need between the director of finance and director of studies with each head of faculty or functional head. Computer equipment is funded centrally on a three or four-yearly 'rolling lease' basis. Common computer software is also funded centrally, with faculties expected to fund any specialist software from their consumable resources.

Functional areas

The functional areas of finance and administration, marketing and operational services, organizational development and curriculum support, each of which is led by a member of the senior management team, prepare proposed expenditure plans for each session and agree budgets with the director of finance following notification from the LSC of funding arrangements. These budgets will include consumable and capital requirements.

Programme area monitoring

All budget holders are monitored against their income and expenditure targets on a monthly basis. Programme area reviews are held termly to discuss ongoing resource and quality issues with each faculty management team. A comprehensive spreadsheet showing the present position is published by the director of finance on the staff intranet.

The role of the corporation

The corporation approves an overall annual budget for income and expenditure and approves capital expenditure proposals following advice from the principal/chief executive. Comprehensive monthly accounts are made available to the members of the corporation finance committee and variations from budget headings discussed at each finance committee meeting as appropriate. Limitations to the principal's authority are laid down in the financial regulations.

Assessing and managing risk

Everything in life of course has some risk attached and the better colleges produce a risk register which analyses what might go wrong and what might prevent the organization from fulfilling its objectives. In a typical scenario, the seriousness of the risk to the organization (1–5), if it were to happen, is multiplied by an estimate of its probability of happening (0–1). Anything with an overall score of above say 2 or 2.5 (the number will vary depending on your corporation's attitude to risk) leads to a possible action plan that will mitigate either the seriousness of that risk or decrease the probability that it will occur. The aim of these actions is to bring the risk down to an acceptable level. If the risk can't be brought down, then the decision may well be taken not to go ahead with the activity. This can be applied to every aspect of the college's operation, from meeting number targets and financial performance to risks of bad industrial relations and adverse publicity. It almost goes without saying that risk assessment is particularly important for curriculum-related activities when students and staff are moving outside the relatively safe college environment. In these cir-cumstances, every care should be taken to ensure that the contribution to the curriculum is significant (otherwise why do it?) and any risk minimal (otherwise don't do it!).

Creating innovation

If you have a stable and happy staff and a tried and tested programme, coupled with a prudent attitude to risk, you should be well on the way to a successful college. Success, however, brings its own risks, not the least of which is a tendency to stick with the tried and tested. To keep the organization moving forward, you need innovation and creativity. This is difficult to achieve. You may be lucky and be surrounded by talented and creative individuals full of new ideas. Or you may not. In which case you have to create a climate in which innovation and creativity can grow.

A good starting point in this is to convince people that mistakes won't lead to some terrible retribution. In fact you may want to make it clear that if people aren't making the odd mistake, then maybe they are not pushing themselves hard enough. Be prepared to set aside a small part of the budget to back new ideas, either by supplying hard cash or buying time to allow what seems like a good idea to be more fully explored. Write down what has changed each year – by college, department, area and course – and encourage each individual to write down, as part of their appraisal, what they have done that is new and different. Publish the results and celebrate the successes widely and often. If you have a staff of 250 and you're not getting at least 500 new ideas/events/changes each year, you need to work harder. Set a creativity/new idea target and treat it as seriously as all the others.

Marketing the product

There are many ways of marketing a college's activities, and the basics of product, price, promotion and place are as true in a college environment as they are in business. The average college, though, serves a variety of different markets. The typical further education college as part of its programme provides vocational and academic qualifications for school leavers and adults, skills and training for employers and non-vocational leisure activities for all. Each segment will need a somewhat different marketing approach. This needs to be based on the benefits that will be derived from the programme, not the programme itself. Not many people want training for training's sake.

Given the reality of ongoing learning being essential for a successful life both in and out of employment, there is also the opportunity/need to build up a long-term relationship with a customer – ideally over a lifetime. Few colleges have grasped this nettle and have a marketing strategy that goes beyond the annual programme or at best the three-year strategic plan. There are some exceptions. There are colleges working with primary schools, for example, and thus investing in a marketing activity that will not pay off for five years or more. None that I know of, however, regard each student as a lifelong customer *and* have active programmes to maintain contact and promote opportunities over decades rather than years. The college that manages to do that will never have to worry about under-recruitment ever again.

Good and successful ideas, of course, abound for each and every area, including the engagement of industrial consultants for each curriculum area to check the relevance of the programme to current needs, free activities and facilities for secondary school pupils and evening accommodation for community groups (meetings/events, etc.). There are DVDs promoting the lifestyle of a student, online prospectuses, Internet walk-throughs of buildings, sample lessons, posters on trains, pull-out newspaper supplements, displays of student work taken around communities, learning buses, scholarships for the gifted and talented, rewards for good performance and attendance, membership schemes and commissioned agents (usually for supplying international students). The list is almost endless. One college even pays 15 year olds at school £5 a time if they will discuss their future career plans with them.

Your real limitation is likely to be the size of your budget rather than a shortage of ideas. As in all communications, though, think about the listener rather than the broadcaster. I know, for example, of a very successful access course that was advertised incredibly cheaply through the personal column of a local paper. 'Bored with life? Looking for a change? Want to meet new people? Try an access course and your life will never be the same again.' The bottom line is that you need to find out what people want and convince them that you are the best organization to supply it. You don't necessarily have to spend a lot of money to do so if you know how to contact them.

Monitoring outcomes

Many years ago as a PhD student researching into the relationship between adult education and community development, I carried out a controlled marketing experiment in

Livingston new town as part of an action research project for the University of Edinburgh. Five brand-new courses were to be offered in the area. Each was advertised in only one very specific way – posters around the town for Course A; a newspaper advert for Course B; for Course C a leaflet drop in a specific and contained postcode area; Course D by verbally telling existing students; and Course E by inclusion in a normal prospectus. When the students came for each course, they were asked how they had heard about it. The answers should have been simple. Unfortunately they weren't as predicted. People had seen courses on posters that weren't there, read about courses in a prospectus in which they weren't included and had a leaflet through their door about a course for which there was no leaflet. The lesson seemed to be that once people have acquired information they really don't remember where it came from. So if you are asking people how they heard about you, don't put your marketing budget on the outcome. It would be a gamble to say the least. Hence there is a commonly held view that 50 per cent of all marketing is probably wasted. Unfortunately, no one really knows which 50 per cent that is.

That's not to say, of course, that all market research is useless – surveys of students and non-students of their views of the college, for example, can be particularly useful – but trying too hard to link cause and effect is almost invariably an over-simplification when there are likely to be other, sometimes unknown, factors at play. The best advice is to employ a good marketing manager who knows the theory and its limitations and has a good idea of the ways in which the various college markets can be addressed. If numbers are rising and positive press coverage in column inches is increasing, and if independent research into individual or employer views of the college show high and increasing levels of satisfaction, then something is working. Usually, though, in FE, it's because you have got a quality product. Without it, all the marketing in the world won't work.

6 Designing a delivery structure

Shapes and sizes

I am not a betting man, but I would be willing to put my shirt on the fact that most new principals/chief executives restructure within the first eighteen months of their appointment. If the college that they have inherited has known 'problems', the timescale is likely to be more like six months to a year.

There are probably two main reasons for this. The first maybe is the need to show that something important is happening now that the new person has arrived and a restructure is a surefire way of demonstrating 'action'. The second is no doubt a belief that the present structure is the root cause of the college's difficulties, whatever they may be. There are some colleges, moreover, that have restructured five times in five years. Unfortunately in many cases the restructure seems to make no real difference and the fundamental problems still remain. The question, of course, is why?

The simple answer is that there is no such thing as a perfect structure that is ideal for any organization. Flat structures, matrices, traditional hierarchies and any of the myriad possible combinations will or will not work, depending on whether or not the right people are doing the right jobs. How the various roles and tasks are packaged together and matched with the skills and interests of the individuals chosen to do them is the key.

In the perfect structure, everyone knows what they have to do to help the organization achieve its goals and they have the skills, power and responsibility to do what they have to do. They also have a degree of independence that does not detract from the team nature of the organization. Designing a structure without taking account of the people involved is almost invariably going to lead to the fitting of square pegs into round holes, with the resulting difficulties that will entail. It makes much more sense to look at the size of the pegs first and shape the holes to fit.

Of course it may be possible to make some new appointments where the fit can be improved by the selection process, but in reality most new leaders or managers will have to work largely with what they have got. Encouragingly in most cases this won't be a problem. Given the size of the average college and the qualifications and experience of its staff, it is highly likely that the skills exist within the organization to move forward. Whether or not this will be reflected in an appropriate structure will depend on the starting point. Building structures around people's skills works. Inventing a structure no matter how logical and trying to fit people into it often doesn't. So rather than launching into a restructuring soon after arrival, it's probably far better to spend your early days really getting to know your people, what they like doing and what they are really good at. The skill then comes in knowing what you need and in matching the two.

Hierarchies

Successful hierarchical structures are usually built around communication links that allow decisions to be taken at the lowest and most appropriate level and encourage information to flow smoothly up and down and across the organization. Pre-computers, there were logistical problems in this that no longer really exist. In the days of the office memo, a practical decision might be 'who needs to know' and copies would wing their way in a few days to the appropriate desk(s). Chains of command were as much about chains of communication as anything else and spans of control were necessarily limited to the number of people you could reasonably talk to or memo.

Today, the all-staff email means that everyone can be informed in seconds. This changes the possibilities of structural design. Structures can be flatter and reporting numbers greater. It also allows less of an excuse for poor communications. If in doubt as to who to tell about a particular activity, why not tell everybody?

Ideally structures should reflect the necessary division of labour for all aspects of the organization's work, matched with the individual's ability to perform them. As a starting point, jobs need to be broken down realistically into a collection of tasks and roles. Analysing the skills of the individuals who are available to carry these out is the next step towards the creation of a successful structure that can be constructed as much from the bottom up as from the top down. With a clear idea of how much time and effort is required for each, workloads can also be better equalized. The problem may be in finding appropriate titles to match the multi-task, multi-roled outcomes.

Remember, too, to allow for some flexibility and an 'exchange mechanism'. A simple example from one college is of senior managers that have their overall responsibilities within the college clearly defined, but exchange responsibilities for specific tasks to play to individual strengths, e.g. the director of marketing has particular project management skills and takes over a critical building project from the director of estates to improve the chances of an on-time completion; the director of curriculum, who has a degree in fine art, leads on the design of the new prospectus instead of the director of marketing.

The relationship between power, skills and responsibilities

The holy grail of structures is one which plays to everyone's strengths and where it is clear as to who is responsible for achieving what and they have the power to reach their goals. It may not be neat or balanced on paper. Where the trinity of power, responsibility and skill do not go together, there is likely to be stress in the individual (How can I possibly be expected to ... when ...?) and lower levels of performance in the organization.

What have you got?

A read through the personnel records of your staff is time well spent for a new leader or senior manager. Very few if any of your staff will have arrived with no experience from elsewhere and the journeys they have taken that have landed them on your shore can be surprising. Yes, there is the job they have been appointed to do, but what else is there buried deep or just below the surface that could be used to make the organization a better or more successful place? Making a list of your staff and the skills that they have identified in their curriculum vitae (CV) that are not being currently used in the organization can give some useful food for thought. If this can be supported by one-to-one discussions of what people would really like to do in the organization, as compared to what they are doing now (possibly discussing a task exchange – giving up something they dislike doing now for something they really enjoy), then it is likely that even more opportunities might become apparent. At this point, you might be in a position to start to think about a more appropriate structure.

Figure 6 Now we've sorted the auditors out perhaps we can get down to some work?

What do you need?

At first glance, asking you to write down what you need to run a successful college or department seems relatively easy. After all, you wouldn't be in the position you're in without some considerable experience. But starting with a blank piece of paper or computer screen every now and again can help you get back to the fundamentals which occasionally get obscured in the hurly-burly of everyday work. A key function of your role as a leader or senior manager is to be able to step outside the 'now' and to reflect. So what do you really want? Hopefully a successful college that has well-designed and marketed programmes that meet needs, are well-resourced with staff, equipment and materials in a safe and attractive environment, and that lead to successful outcomes for those who participate in them. So far so good, but then comes the task of relating this back to a delivery structure and the people you've got. Pretty much every word opens up a raft of questions that need to be answered before you can begin. What's a well-designed programme? How should it best be marketed? How are needs to be identified? Unless you have spent some time thinking about these issues you are not really in a position to move forward. To free up your thinking, you might want to turn the existing structure upside down into an inverted triangle. The principal/chief executive and senior management team would be at the base, skilled support staff in the centre, and the highly trained front-line staff who deliver the product to the students at the top.

If you still feel unsure as to what you need, there are another 500 or so colleges in the UK alone who are grappling with the same questions, some of whom will be well ahead of where you are at the moment on whatever aspect you are considering. Too many leaders and managers try to re-invent not only the wheel but the whole car. Set aside at least a small proportion of each week to find better practice elsewhere. It'll not only save you considerable time in the medium to long term – it will probably prevent you from making mistakes that you will regret.

What do you want?

What you need to do to improve the performance of your organization for the present, however, is only part of the picture. As a leader, you have not been appointed to maintain the status quo. You have been appointed to move the organization forward. Unfortunately no one has given you a crystal ball and the future is uncertain. How do you avoid being successful today because your organization is well adapted to the environment and falling behind tomorrow as you fail to keep up with the necessary changes? The dinosaur no doubt enjoyed his day but . . .

The answer lies in making sure that your organization is comfortable in a changing environment and accepts change as the new steady state. Arguably, you have to make sure that some things are constantly changing even if they don't have to so that your people are used to adapting and are therefore better prepared when bigger and/or more necessary changes appear on the horizon. The skill lies in pacing these changes so that they do not appear threatening and people improve their adaptability bit by bit. Think of it as starting a fitness programme. Put someone in a gym for an hour and send them on a five-mile run: if they've spent the last five years as a couch potato it will probably kill them. Build up their fitness over a period of months starting with what they can do and, stretching them little by little, in time the gym/run scenario will be achieved with comparative ease.

It's often said that most people don't like change, but it's more likely that they don't like the consequences of change rather than change itself. Otherwise, why would millions go on holiday abroad every year for a rest where everything from the sunshine to the food and the culture is different? Good structures and good jobs should have the ability to accommodate changes within them as part of the normal process of life. You may not want to introduce changes from Day 1 for the reasons suggested earlier, but sooner or later change has to become the status quo.

Changing personnel

Having spent time considering what you've got, what you need and what you want, you are almost invariably going to be able to spot at least one situation, and probably more than one, which could significantly be improved by a change of personnel. Let's work on a not uncommon scenario that you have a senior member of staff who is not delivering, in your view, what he or she needs to deliver to contribute to the success of the organization. A common response in this situation is to restructure the person out or appoint new blood while moving them to one side. While there are occasions when either of these might work, be aware of the dangers of both. Have you really got to the bottom of why things are not working out as you feel they should be? Are you sure, for example, that the person is the problem? Have they the skills, power and responsibility to do what you want them to do or would they be more successful doing something else? How confident are you (based on facts rather than gut instinct) that your new solution will work? What messages will be received by the rest of the organization by your actions? And perhaps most importantly, what happens if the changes make the situation no better or even worse?

Proceed carefully and spend time and effort bottoming the problem. There aren't too many people in further education who are not trying to do a good job and are merely turning up each day to earn money. More frequently, the problem lies in poor systems and inadequate training. The most common mistake is to act too quickly. Analysing the problem, discussing it with others with relevant experience and above all with the individual whom you have identified as being the source, is a very obvious course of action, but one which is often avoided in jumping from problem identification to believing/hoping that there is a simple solution – a change of personnel and all will be well.

A look at the history of management information systems (MIS) and their staff in colleges can provide a good example of the kinds of problems that can arise. In the early 1990s, many MIS staff were replaced or moved on because their college's management information systems were not working. It was assumed that the managers were just not up to it, when in fact the real problem lay outside their control. The essence of most college's MIS problems was not incompetent MIS managers or inadequate systems, but the almost total lack of training for lecturers as to the importance of the new systems. They simply did not understand how the funding of the organization worked and the basic need for 100 per cent accuracy in recording what a student was doing. The new world was a far cry from the paper-based register system and the very rough count of student numbers that existed before incorporation. 'Rubbish in, rubbish out' was the most common error and legions of register coordinators, MIS managers, faculty assistants and funding analysts were not going to make matters better until the grass-roots problem was addressed. This meant coding each course correctly, recording every student activity accurately and the painstaking matching of local and central records until everyone could agree as to what was happening. Suddenly, MIS managers and systems no longer had a shelf life of months, their skills could be appreciated and senior managers were able to concentrate on the more important parts of their business.

Avoiding common pitfalls

Talk to the average college leader about who the most important people in his or her college are, and I would be surprised if you didn't receive the answer 'the students'. Look at the structure of the average college and ask whose needs does it most reflect, and the answer is probably 'the staff'. A good exercise is to look at your structure and concentrate on the posts that make the most impact on the students and their experience. Is everything important covered? Have you got the right balance of skills and the right numbers of people in these posts? Or is the structure more reflective of the administrative and bureaucratic needs of the education system? When you've thought this through and redesigned your structure so that it fully reflects the needs of the students and not the requirements of a bureaucracy, you're on the way to becoming a national hero.

Balancing stability and the need for change

In a constantly changing environment, jobs and structures will themselves need to change to reflect the new challenges and opportunities that the world offers. Experience shows that evolution tends to be a more acceptable and pleasant way of changing than the structural revolutions that some colleges have endured, often with greater frequency than South American republics. Looking systematically at functions or areas which can be improved on a cyclical basis is a sensible compromise approach, with a more regular review of those which impact most directly on the student and the key performance indicators of the institution (normally student-related as well). Pretty well everyone can accept a new role or way of working, provided it is clear why it is needed and that there are likely to be benefits.

7 Providing resources

Sources of income

Sources and the extent of income from each source will vary from college to college, although, for all, the underpinning key customer is likely to be the Learning and Skills Council (LSC) who will fund between 50 per cent and 80 per cent of its provision. In essence, there is a contract for delivering a plan, with payments following student numbers and penalties for losing students early or for students who do not achieve. More recently, the degree of certainty from year to year has begun to be reduced, as new entrants to the FE market are being encouraged and there is a percentage reduction in the college allocation year on year to be re-bid for in the pursuit of specific government objectives.

An important consideration for any college, therefore, must be to maximize its LSC income. The most obvious way is to increase the number of new students enrolled and, subject to LSC agreements, to attract additional funding. There are, however, potentially easier ways of achieving the same objective.

First and foremost of these is to retain a greater percentage of students to the end of their programme. This involves a good understanding as to why students leave and hence some time and effort following up early departures. Evidence from elsewhere would suggest that problems with the college programme are rarely the key issue − a tribute perhaps to improved guidance and admissions procedures in matching the right student with the right course, and rising standards of teaching and learning. Of much greater importance is what happens in the early days at college. First and foremost is the need for students to feel comfortable in their new environment and to make friends. Hence carefully designed inductions that aim to achieve this are a must.

Secondly, there are the problems associated with missing classes and falling behind with work, sometimes to the extent that leaving seems to be the only option. Tight monitoring of attendance and progress is essential and a good tutorial system can be worth its weight in gold. Set minimum standards of performance (e.g. 85 per cent attendance) and insist on all work being in on time, with consequences of various kinds if these are not met, including extra holiday work if necessary. Nag if you have to and don't let the problem go beyond the point of no return if you can help it.

A third important factor is funding. Can students afford to stay on at college, given the temptations of the money provided by a job? In recent years of relatively high employment this has been less of a problem, with most students in further education working part-time while carrying on with their studies. The introduction of education maintenance allowances in 2004 has also helped. In some cases, however, especially where students are drawn from economically disadvantaged groups, more specific action may be necessary, including the need to redraw the timetable to make part-time working easier (full-time courses, perhaps, being compressed into three days of college attendance). You may even want to consider employing students within the college under an 'earn as you learn' scheme.

For the students who successfully complete their programmes, the opportunity for the college to extend their studies to a higher level or to take an alternative supportive qualification (the commercial equivalent of building on customer loyalty) is rarely fully exploited. How many colleges offer reduced fees for repeat business, for example? Most seem to recruit from scratch each year.

Other contracts that will figure largely in a college's total income are likely to be those for subsets of government funding including, at present, work-based learning, employer training, non-vocational provision and higher education.

Next comes fees – and here the variation from college to college is considerable. LSC funding assumes at present a certain fee element built in, but there are still colleges which are reluctant to push too hard in this direction. If you have just been appointed to the top post, this is an area which warrants early attention. At the very least, there should be a clear policy as to why certain fees are being charged and a sensible policy for special concessions. A good starting point is a base rate per taught hour – which could then be enhanced to cover special services or respond to market opportunities. Remember, if it's too cheap, there is often an assumption of poor quality.

There are then the commercial opportunities that colleges can exploit. There may be catering facilities which produce a restaurant income or maybe even ready meals for sale to busy staff and students, shops (supporting retailing students), perhaps a travel agency (travel and tourism), hair and beauty salons, fitness centres, a sports hall for hire, garages (motor vehicle), nurseries and, in the case of specialist agricultural colleges, even garden centres and farm shops.

Less obvious perhaps are the opportunities to 'sell' the college's infrastructure – especially if you have surplus accommodation. Possibilities include renting space to other training organizations or providing supportive facilities for start-up businesses. There are also college products that might be sold, including, for example, student artwork, pieces made in the joinery workshop, or Web design services, to name but three. In the end, a college is a business and it's your job to make sure that income-generating opportunities are not wasted.

There are lessons to be learned here from the American community colleges, where raising money is an important issue. Appointed bid writers and fundraisers are commonplace – effectively people whose sole job it is to make money – and there are also those who build on the power and money of ex-students through the establishment of alumni organizations and the encouragement of donations. It might be a long-term policy, but there are even those whose job is to encourage legacy funding through wills.

Main items of expenditure

Having established your level of income, you now come to the point where you have to decide how to spend it. It's important here to bear Mr Micawber in mind – and, given the accuracy with which you need to be able to forecast your student numbers to secure your LSC funding, the distance between happiness and misery is a very narrow one.

Start by allowing yourself a margin of error. Take 2 per cent off the total budget and allocate it to a 'contingency' line. Pretend you haven't got it and draw up your expenditure plans accordingly. At the end of the year if it's still there, it gives you the opportunity either of a major saving or of a major investment – the refurbishment of an area perhaps.

Next, identify what you have to spend (virtually no choice). Include in this staff costs for all those on permanent contracts, rates, gas, electricity, telephone, etc. and you will find that you will probably have already spent well over 80 per cent of your budget. Look at what you've got left and build up from the bottom what your experts feel they need to spend on, for example, marketing, routine maintenance and student materials, where you do have some choice. If this comes to more than you have left, go around again and if necessary again and again until everyone faces up to the reality and has a budget that is based on a level of activity that you can afford. Never assume that any shortfall can be made up by increasing income unless you are 100 per cent sure of the source. Allocate these budgets to a small number of individuals (management level) and hold them responsible for keeping to those budgets. Make it clear to the finance section that no order can be approved if it takes a budget holder over budget without your express written permission (eating into the contingency) and make it equally clear to everyone else that not keeping to their budgets will result in death at dawn by firing squad or earlier if they are available. Publish the results so that everyone can see who has got what, what it's for and why.

Having gone through this process thoroughly once, you have the opportunity to lock in your expenditure in terms of a percentage of the total budget (e.g. 5 per cent to buildings maintenance, 2 per cent to marketing, 3 per cent to leasing, including computer leasing or whatever) at least for the period of your plan. You can then concentrate on the main business in hand without having sleepless nights over whether you can afford it.

For both income and expenditure, it is useful to distinguish between what is relatively permanent funding (and you can include higher education and LSC funding within these categories) and the passing temporary funds of the latest initiatives (e.g. European social funding). Don't allocate permanent resources to temporarily funded projects unless you are very clear as to what will happen to those resources when the initiative bandwagon moves on to the next idea. Above all, don't build expectations that you or the college will be able to pick up the tab when the specialist money has disappeared. Too many colleges have found themselves holding some very important and expensive babies when project funding has ceased. Have an exit strategy before you start.

Figure 7 Are you sure you need paper to teach? Money is scarce, you know.

Finally, don't neglect the estate. Not only does it have to be systematically maintained (and a five-year maintenance plan is probably worth commissioning if you haven't already got one)

but it also needs to be improved to keep up with the continually rising expectations of staff and students. This needs to
be factored into the budget from the outset. Generally speaking, you want to improve both the efficiency of space utilization and raise the specifications within that space. Central
timetabling matched with local ownership thereafter is essential
if you are not to suffer from 'space creep', whereby everyone
books some extra space 'just in case ...'. Spare space can be
used to improve the social areas of both staff and students.
Always allow a sum of money each year to upgrade at least one
staff room as a sure-fire way of improving morale. Similarly,
aim to employ caretaking staff who can mend leaking taps, put
up shelves, plaster the odd piece of wall and paint to an
acceptable standard. You may have to pay them more, but it
will be money well spent.

Characteristics of efficient and inefficient colleges

At the time of incorporation, when figures were first published
as to the cost per FTE student by college, the difference
between the most and least efficient was in the region of 300
per cent. Even if you accounted in the most generous way
possible for all local issues and special case pleas, some colleges
were at least twice as expensive as others in delivering broadly
the same curriculum.

This was largely the result of local authority control and the
different importance that local politicians put on their colleges.
Data as to performance and indeed student numbers were very
limited and the determination of the college's budget each year
was largely the result of negotiation and politics, starting with
the historical information available from the year before.
Without a mechanism for sharing this information nationally,
it's hardly surprising that over a period of time divergences
became greater.

The removal of colleges from local authority control and
their establishment as independent corporations and the
emergence of the Further Education Funding Council (FEFC)
as essentially a funding body began to change this world

forever. When the figures were looked at nationally, there were obviously some Local Education Authorities (LEAs) who had been very generous and some that had been equally mean. The painful process of 'convergence' began, as funds were gradually moved away from the high earners to those less fortunate, although eight years later as the FEFC passed into history, so wide had the gap been and so difficult had many colleges found it to cut back, that the process was still not complete.

For those at the bottom end of the spectrum, who dreamed of a land of milk and honey as money flowed towards them from the better off, there were some small adjustments upwards (a safety net baseline of funding, for example, was set for some 30 colleges) but the opportunity was taken nationally to look for efficiency gains. It was quickly realized that some colleges were managing fine with half the money of others and, as the first inspection reports emerged, that there was no link between quality and funding.

First in the firing line was staffing and, in particular, what were interpreted as generous conditions of service for teaching staff (The Silver Book). There followed a long battle over new contracts which, in particular, contained increased teaching hours and a reduced holiday entitlement. Given that pay and conditions prior to incorporation were negotiated nationally and were basically the same for all institutions, a moment's reflection should have been enough for everyone to have realized that the differences were such that this could not really be at the heart of the problem.

For whatever reason, however, this was the battleground on which the first drive for efficiency was fought. Definitions of teaching and non-teaching time were clarified, annual hours were increased by, on average, 15 per cent, and holidays were almost halved. The atmosphere was poisonous.

Almost 15 years on, the gaps still exist between the rich and the poor and salaries for teachers vary widely from college to college, despite national recommendations each year from the Association of Colleges (AoC). Interestingly enough, the college with arguably the best pay and conditions for teaching and support staff, nationally, is also one of the best in performance terms and has Grade A financial status. In considering efficiency and effectiveness, therefore, there must be other and more important factors at play.

If we stay with staffing issues for the moment – after all it represents somewhere between 65 and 70 per cent of the average college budget – there are clearly colleges that operate better than others. It's not generally the teaching hours per full-time lecturer or the number of holiday days, however, that make the difference. The answer lies elsewhere.

The first place to look is at the number and grading of support staff – i.e. those who do not directly teach or who are not directly involved in student learning. Here the variations between colleges are enormous. Some colleges have ratios in excess of 1.5 to 1 of support to teaching staff, with little or no evidence of better performance or higher levels of service. Look at your support staff numbers and structures in the cold light of day and ask yourself a simple question: 'If I was running the college as my own private company, how many of these posts would I need to fund?' Bearing in mind that you would be paying for them, what would your answer be? The same number as you have at present? I doubt it.

Another interesting area to consider is 'management' efficiency. Even in colleges with identical structures, this could vary. Consider the case of two colleges, for example, each with five heads of faculty, each of whom is paid the same. Do they have equal faculty management costs? Not if, for example, in one college the heads of faculty teach for six hours a week each and in the other they don't. There's a £50,000 annual difference to start with.

If you want to set a baseline for improving your efficiency, add up all the contractual time of all your staff (i.e. the 37 hours or whatever on each contract). Add up all the teaching hours in their contracts, take a deep breath and work out how many support hours there are for each teaching hour. Then work on reducing it.

A good start in this respect is by looking at tasks that the college needs to have done rather than jobs that individuals currently hold. Here are two simple examples. A college has an administrator attached to each faculty. Do they have to operate from a separate office? Could they do their work equally well while supervising a learning resource centre? Or be based in reception? Could they be first-aid trained or be involved in training business studies students? Would it be better to pay one person more to cover these tasks or employ two people?

Or how about investing in an online enrolment system and reducing the number of extra staff that have to be paid in August and September each year? How many staff are doing administrative jobs that really should be computerized?

In many cases, however, support staffing is not the real problem. The biggest potential efficiencies come from the organization of the core business, i.e. the curriculum. In this respect, the key issue in most colleges and the one that makes the greatest difference to efficiency is class sizes.

Let's leave aside for a moment arguments of when is a class not a class and let's use an old-fashioned definition of a teacher in a classroom with a group of students (forgetting for the moment learning support, student assisted learning, e-learning, blended learning and all the rest). Reading through any inspection report on an FE or ACL institution for the past four years suggests that there are average class sizes of less than 12 in the majority of colleges. Increase that in your organization to, say, 15, and you have a 25 per cent efficiency gain. What's more, there is no evidence to suggest that students perform better in smaller rather than larger groups. Given the percentage of your budget spent on teaching staff, that represents a million pound plus 'opportunity' in the average college. So why doesn't it happen?

First and foremost, many colleges are maybe being too ambitious in trying to offer a truly comprehensive curriculum across a wide geographical area and at all times of the day (and sometimes night). A glance at the average prospectus will reveal not only a plethora of minority interest provision, but many classes duplicated in different locations and at different times. That's fine – if that's what you want to do and you can afford it. If it's not, it's a usually a major area from which you will be able to release resources for other things.

Start by looking at any split group or any class that is offered more than once in a week. Calculate realistically what would happen if there were no splits and no duplications. Yes, student numbers and income will fall, but in most, if not all, cases, the potential savings far outweigh these drops. Let's take a situation in which each full-time student produces an income of £4,000 for a college and a lecturer who teaches for 24 hours a week costs £32,000 a year, including on-costs. A typical scenario might be one in which a full-time class group recruits, say, 26 people (too many for the room) and is split into two. If, say, the group is taught for 16 hours a week, this represents an increase in teaching costs of 16/24 × £32,000 or £21,000. Closing the class as 'full' at 24 (maximum room size) loses £8,000 in income, but produces a net 'saving' over the split-group scenario of £13,000 – and that's just for one class. Or what about a GCSE English class offered in three different locations in the evenings with, say, 10 students in each? What happens if only one class is offered? More people have to travel and numbers may fall but the provision is still available and savings will have been made. These are not easy or popular issues to address but if you are in financial difficulty you may have very little choice.

The third main component of savings in the classroom revolves around, in its simplest terms, the number of hours that students are taught. For this, a somewhat more sophisticated analysis is needed. Is the aim to teach the students for a certain amount of time (scenario A) or is it to have the students *learning* for a certain amount of time (scenario B) – and how do the number and type of resources for scenario A compare with those for scenario B? What is the optimum blend of resources (including teaching time) to produce the required results and can a 'blended learning approach' be cheaper and more effective than the traditional teacher/student relationship? There are no easy answers, but the introduction of new technologies and the increased opportunities that they bring, together with a changing of thinking away from teaching and the teacher as the font of all knowledge to learning and the student as the receptor of a variety of inputs, offers considerable scope for not only cheaper, but more effective educational provision.

Add to the above common timetabling, allowing students to mix and match modules or activities from across the whole curriculum (to allow, for example, caterers and child care students to take first aid together), and a close look at the curriculum is likely to produce far more efficiency gains than those deriving from making staff work longer hours. This is a real challenge for senior managers. Can they get better results with everyone working less?

Benchmarking calculations and ratios

So what figures should be of particular interest to you? The number of students who start a programme, complete it and are successful are key, but of more use when the figures can be seen over a period of time (say, three or four years) and benchmarked against similar programmes in other colleges. Similarly, the average class size per teaching hour for a programme, an area and the college as a whole, subdivided into full-time, part-time and full-time equivalent (FTE). The number of hours of teaching per student. The number of contracted teaching hours for staff and the number actually delivered. The costs per FTE student – staffing and non-staffing. The income earned by each FTE student. The amount of total time spent on teaching and on non-teaching activities (to avoid 'support creep'!). Student retention and pass rates by area. The amount of income generated by each major contributor to the college budget (again, trends are particularly important) and the amount of income that is at risk through contracts not being renewed or coming to a natural end. There are many others.

The list is a long one, but you don't need to look at all of these every day or even every week. It is, however, worth spending some time working out what you do want to look at when. The key time is the time when you can still influence the outcome. Hence student applications for next year probably need to be considered on a weekly or even a daily basis, because marketing activities can be stepped up if unsatisfactory comparisons begin to emerge. If you look at the applications also in terms of the courses being applied for and the areas from which the applications are coming, on the basis of calculated conversion rates this will give you a pretty accurate prediction of student numbers well before enrolment.

Staff turnover and sickness rates, on the other hand, are probably only worth a good look annually, as there may be any number of special factors that can't be changed on a day-to-day basis or influences beyond your control. At least, decide on what you are going to look at when, how you are going to examine the results and, above all, what you can or will do if the figures are not to your liking.

Dealing with inherited problems and recovery situations

It's not impossible of course, or indeed unusual, to find yourself in a situation where you have taken over from a recently departed leader and the whole place is in what can only be described as a bit of a mess. This usually involves a combination of falling student numbers, poor success rates, low staff morale and a large and increasing budget deficit – the nightmare scenario. In the words of *Dad's Army*'s Corporal Jones, 'Don't panic'.

The first thing you should try to do is prevent the situation from becoming any worse. If the problem is primarily a financial one, centralize control of all expenditure under your personal authority and 'freeze' everything in sight – promotions, new posts, jobs in the pipeline – unless you personally are convinced that the expenditure is absolutely essential. To use an analogy, if you have a burst pipe, the first thing to do is turn off the water supply.

Secondly, get an assessment as to how bad the situation really is (usually at least 25 per cent and more frequently 50 per cent worse than you were first led to believe) and, as soon as possible, share this information and what you intend to do about it with your staff (or at least your first steps). At this point, you have a great opportunity not only to share the information but to share the problem and its solution. To do so, you will have to take on board the fact that your staff are human and subject to Maslow's hierarchy of needs (Maslow 1954). If you can promise them the security of not losing their jobs and still being able to pay their mortgages, then there's every chance that they will quickly get behind you. This may seem difficult but, given natural rates of turnover, in return for the staff being flexible as to what they do (e.g. if a receptionist leaves, a librarian might need to fill in on reception) this is almost always possible. Just look at the basic sums – a college with a £20 million budget and 5 per cent staff turnover (a very low figure, incidentally – for most colleges the figure is likely to be something in excess of 10 per cent and for colleges in trouble even higher), the staffing bill will be in the region of £13 million–£14 million. Non-replacement of that 5 per cent gives a potential saving of £700,000. Allowing for the 'must haves', where no possible alternative to a replacement can be found, there's half a million a year towards the problem before you start. With a higher staff turnover figure, this can approach a million and you're well on your way.

If the problem is qualitative rather than financial, then solutions are probably much easier. What is needed here is an analysis of every aspect of the student's contact with the college, from enquiry through to leaving, as to what is exactly being done, alongside what might be done, drawing from best practice scenarios elsewhere. A 'student cycle' analysis is required: enquiry, application, interview, pre-enrolment activity, enrolment, induction, attendance policies, teaching and learning, attitudes to set work, learning and personal support mechanisms, monitoring and tutorial practices, examination preparation, destination analysis, follow up and repeat business. Usually, finding solutions to quality problems like this is more about making changes to ways of doing things than spending money. A similar 'staff cycle' approach can also be employed (enquiry, application, selection, pre-induction, induction, mentoring, support, target setting, aspects of the job, appraisal, training, moving on) by asking how things are being done at present at each point and why what is recognized as best practice elsewhere can't be substituted. It's surprising what will come to light. Once again, sharing the problem and asking for solutions will not only get staff involved, but also is much more likely to produce a successful outcome.

Investing for the future

By concentrating on the here and now when there are immediate and serious problems to be solved, this does not mean that as the leader you should not also be looking into the future to a time when the current troubles are behind you and the college is on an even keel. This is difficult, but, if at all possible, what you are putting in place to get out of the current difficulty should be forming firmer foundations for the years ahead. One of the challenges of the job, even in normal circumstances, is that there will be times when you will find yourself working in three time zones – looking backwards and analysing the previous years' out-turns and the lessons that can be learnt; dealing with the present; and looking a year or more ahead, planting now the seeds that will blossom some time in the future. Balancing these requirements is once again as much an art as a science but this process can be helped by allocating a small amount of diary time each month to a study of the college's historical performances and an attempt at crystal-ball gazing as to what might be in store.

Aiming for an 'in year' surplus of anywhere between two per cent and three per cent is a good start in providing the financial backing for those as yet unseen future developments. If these are to include a new capital spend, then this surplus should be set at least at the level of servicing the debt necessary for such a development. Otherwise, where's the money going to come from? Listing this as a contingency in the budget also covers the possibility that you may not have got this year completely right and you have something to fall back on. It's a good idea to work on the assumption that life isn't totally predictable and to budget and act accordingly.

Investing in the future, though, is more than providing the funds for an improved infrastructure and possible new provision. It's also about investing in your staff both to deal with issues of succession planning and developing their skills so that their contribution to the organization can increase with their experience.

8 Dealing with people

Dealing with the powers that be and would like to be – stakeholders and board members

There are times when I think it must be really easy running a large business. All you have to do is make a profit and keep the shareholders happy. Life is not so easy for the college leader. Not only do they have to do both of these (for profit substitute surplus and for shareholders substitute students) but they also need to keep everyone else happy who has an interest in what the college is doing. There's the local community (car parking and the neighbours), politicians, local and national, funding bodies, examination organizations, employers, schools, staff, board members, inspectors, the press, etc., all of whom at some point or another will have a view to what the institution should be doing. What's more, they all have a *legitimate* interest in such matters, such is the importance of the average college to the community.

Given this plethora of demands, if you have a genuine desire to satisfy them all, you are probably wondering where to start. Begin by taking the initiative and being proactive in these relationships. Think about what these people need from you and the college in normal times (rather than when a particular issue arises) and arrange to meet those needs accordingly. It's useful to keep the local MP on board, for example, and the offering of a meeting once a year to update them on what the college is doing and where it's going is probably sufficient. If some aspect of FE suddenly becomes a national issue, they know where to come – and you know where to go. For local politicians, the possibility of an annual visit, a discussion and a lunch usually goes down well. This, of course, is in addition to any invitations to college events that you may feel are appropriate.

For key customers – employers, schools and possibly some community groups – a more detailed marketing strategy is needed, but once again it pays to be on the front foot – otherwise the only time you are likely to hear from some of these people is when there is a problem and you have no relationship base on which to build to help find a solution.

The board members, of course, are in a slightly different league. They are, after all, responsible for key aspects of the organization and they need to be regularly informed and involved in the college's activities. Discuss with the clerk how they intend to do this and what help they need from you. Don't try and do this yourself – otherwise you are in danger of muddying the waters between management and governance.

Deciding on the staff mix

Colleges are relatively complicated organizations that are constantly changing. Education and training needs change, areas grow and decline, expectations of what should be available to support students and their learning seem to be continually rising. The challenge for college leaders and managers is to balance this state of flux with a relatively stable workforce that can deliver what is required. In this respect, an early question to ask is what do you need 'permanently' and what would be better provided on a subcontracted and short-term basis?

Colleges respond in different ways to this challenge. Some like to employ all their staff for all their functions, increasing their level of control, but at some increased risk. There is then a continuum of subcontracting – from those that farm out their catering, cleaning and grounds maintenance to those who also rely on one or more third-party providers to supply significant percentages of their teaching staff. Indeed, there is very little that isn't subcontracted out by somebody – from MIS to finance. In the end, it's a balancing decision. Subcontracting tends to be more expensive, but usually – and in the best of cases, always – is fully backed up (i.e. if someone leaves, the service continues seamlessly).

Some control, however, is invariably handed over and if the quality declines, it isn't always easy to get corrective action. Personally, I don't think it's sensible to hand over control of too much of the core business (i.e. the student teaching and learning) although some percentage of part-time, third-party provider staff reduces the risk of being left with staff with the 'wrong' qualifications and experience if demands change. In the present environment, it is probably a sensible policy to have somewhere in the region of 15 per cent of your teaching hours in this category that can be relatively easily changed or if necessary 'switched off'. Quality may be reduced from what could be achieved if you did not have to rely on part-timers in this way, but sometimes you may have to trade some quality for reduced risk. This is not an easy decision to make. There are no right or wrong answers but there are consequences that will change the way in which you need to operate.

When considering whether or not to take someone onto the permanent staff, you need to be confident that either the job will still be there in the future or the person will be able to adapt and take on a different role. This is likely to vary from area to area and according to how certain you are as to the ongoing nature of the business you are considering. As a rule of thumb in today's world, if you see nothing likely to change in five years, you can probably treat it as if it were permanent. Finance directors are safe; teachers of shorthand well on the way to extinction. If in doubt, short-term contracts or consultancies for specific projects may be a better way forward.

Complicating matters is the rise of the computer, the Internet and virtual learning environments in their importance to the student learning experience. We are still some way off teachers and lecturers being re-branded as learning guides but those starting their careers today as full-time lecturers will have very different roles in the course of their career. Can you even say, for example, what their jobs might look like in five years' time, given the pace of technological change? An important characteristic of all college appointees therefore needs to be adaptability and flexibility, and more blended posts are likely to emerge alongside blended learning provision as the importance of the lecturer as the font of all knowledge declines and their steering/guiding role increases.

Selecting staff

Selecting staff is one of the most important tasks that a college undertakes and any manager worth his or her salt will go to any amount of trouble to get it right. The investment involved is significant – and getting it wrong can be really expensive, not only in monetary terms but in the effects on students' lives and the performance and the reputation of the college. Appointing a lecturer, say, at the age of 30 and with a retirement age of say 65 is a £1 million plus commitment in today's money. It is certainly worth more attention than a few questions in the context of a 20-minute interview.

The starting point, however, goes back way beyond the advertising and selection process to the point where a vacancy or the need for a new appointment is first identified. This very important part of the process is frequently rushed through. Harry leaves. We need to replace Harry. Or do we? Question 1 is 'Do we really need a replacement (or perhaps a better question for a public servant, if I was spending my own money, would I still be doing this and in this way?)'. Question 2 is 'Are we looking for a clone of the person who has just gone, or do we really need something a bit (or possibly a lot) different?'

New or replacement posts are times of opportunity. They are times when the skills mix of those left in the organization needs to be reviewed so that the replacement/new appointment complements and adds to what is already in the pot and does not just replace what has been taken out. It's a time for improvement, not maintaining the status quo.

Having decided that a post is needed (it's passed the personal money test) the next step is to produce a full and accurate job description. What exactly do you want the person to do and what are the essential and desirable skills/characteristics of the person to be appointed? Be careful here. Essential means essential. If a person doesn't possess the essential skills, then they shouldn't even be applying, let alone be short-listed. Too many essentials and you won't have an appointment. None and you

Figure 8 Don't you think you're expecting a lot from the candidate? After all we're only recruiting an English teacher.

really haven't thought through the job you want doing and you might as well be recruiting from the local bus stop.

Now comes the search for a suitable person. There are many ways in which the initial search can be done. Advertising is the most usual, but once again there are opportunities and pitfalls. Firstly, are you advertising in the right place (i.e. in the place where your potential applicants will see it) and, secondly, have you worded your advertisement in such a way that it stands out from the crowd and really sells your college as the place to be? Far too little time is spent on this aspect of many adverts. This is surprising when you consider that all words cost the same, good ones and bad ones, negatives and positives. Look at the last advert your college produced for a lecturer. Compare it with others at the same time. Does it emphasize your organization's USPs (unique selling points), which may include favourable location factors such as affordable housing and that it is within reach of areas of outstanding natural beauty, as well as the remuneration and benefits package? Is it the best you can do? If not, why not? Remember that to become or remain successful, you have to be able to attract the best talent.

Of course, you can use specialist recruitment agencies for this first part of the process, but unless it's a very senior post of a specialist nature there will probably be sufficient expertise in the college to do it yourself.

Before the enquiries start arriving, however, have you decided exactly how they are going to be handled? From the telephone, letter, email contact onwards, your response will speak volumes about the college. Is there an application form and is it specific to the job or just a standard one? Is the information sent to applicants who are interested in applying tailored, professional and relevant? Is it personalized? Above all, ask yourself if the pack you are sending out landed on your mat, would you be impressed or depressed? This is a real marketing opportunity for the college. Treat it as such.

Hopefully you have given all these issues some thought, but there are other issues that you need to address before the applications arrive. The obvious question is what are you going to do with them and, assuming you attract a reasonable number, how are you going to arrive at a short list? It certainly helps here to use the essential and desirable characteristics as a checklist in this regard and add any other factors that you have decided are important before you look at the first application. A short-listing team should be appointed and ideally a list of between five and seven candidates selected for further contact. This allows for dropouts and a possible choice of one from three or four at the final stages.

From now on it gets serious. You have a small number of candidates who all appear to be suitable for the job in question and you need to pick one. Personally, I know of no system that will guarantee that the best person for the job will be appointed. There are too many unique factors present in the final stages – perhaps the best person is off colour, or the chemistry between the candidate and panel members just doesn't work. But there are ways in which you can pretty well ensure that you will appoint someone who is at least competent for the post in hand.

Perhaps the least useful of these is references – certainly since the onset of the *Data Protection Act* and the right of individuals to see what is written about them. General 'Tell me about so and so' approaches are pretty well useless, but a targeted series of questions seeking factual clarifications can be helpful if the responses are received before an appointment is offered. There's no reason of course why these questions from the referee should not go beyond the 'How many days absence has Mr X had in the last year?' to 'Could you describe Mr X's involvement in Project X (which from the application seems to have be delivered single-handedly)?' In other words, personalize the request and aim to increase your knowledge of the suitability of the candidate before the final stages, when you have to make a decision.

Of more use are skills tests set for short-listed candidates. These are practical tasks to test that an applicant can really do what they claim they can do. For teachers, these are relatively easy to devise. Ask them, for example, to bring with them their current schemes of work and to teach a group of students or staff on a set topic for 20 minutes or so. If you're not impressed, don't appoint. If they can't produce an exciting and interesting learning experience for 20 minutes with advance notice for a job they want, what hope is there for a good performance 24 hours a week, week in week out? Ask them also to bring evidence of the recent exam results for the students they have taught and compare them against national benchmarks. Even where there might be reasons for significant variations, positive or negative, they will invariably form the basis of an interesting discussion.

Support staff can also be put through their paces in a similar way. Presenting a marketing strategy for a basic skills campaign in the local community, analysing and commenting on opportunities within a college budget are both useful exercises, depending on the job that is being offered. So is the taking of notes from a meeting and producing action minutes for an administrative appointment, or the repairing of a leaking tap for that caretaker role.

During all this time, however, be constantly aware that selection is a two-way process. You want to choose the best person for the job, but you need them to choose your organization as one in which they want to work. You are buying and selling at the same time. Every aspect of the process should be professional and show your organization in the best light.

Finally, there comes the moment of truth. Who are you going to appoint? It's best not to leave candidates waiting around interminably for a decision. This can be potentially unpleasant and embarrassing. It is far better to speak to the candidates by phone the next day, starting with your first choice. You may then be able to work your way down the list if they say no without anyone realizing their place in the pecking order. Once you have made an appointment, always give feedback to unsuccessful candidates as to why they were not appointed on this occasion and how you feel they might improve in the future. Remember you want them to feel they have been well treated by the college. They or their colleagues may be back!

There are then two further aspects to the appointment process — induction and probation. For a successful appointment, the newcomer needs a well thought-through and thorough introduction to the organization — ideally spread over a period of time — that allows them to grow into the job and quickly become a fully contributing member of the team. Appointing a mentor can help, but mentors really need a 'job description' and training if you want their role to go beyond that of 'being there if needed'.

New staff from outside the organization also have a unique role to play in the first few months of their appointment. They are fresh eyes and will, if encouraged, be able to spot flaws or peculiarities that old hands have overlooked. I remember one college principal, who had invested the equivalent of the national debt in a new reception area at the time of incorporation, asking a newcomer for their honest opinion of what they thought of the entrance to the college. He was shocked when the newcomer said they weren't impressed. Yes, the new building work was fine, but the first five notices/signs they had seen as they approached told them to go away! (Reserved parking only — No students beyond this point, etc.). The principal admitted that he had been coming in through that entrance for years and the signs had never registered. A few easy changes and, for that college at least, a giant leap forward for public relations.

Most posts have a probationary period, but rarely has much thought been given to the way in which this period should be used. It really is an opportunity to make sure that the person you have appointed can do the job to your satisfaction. Hence a careful monitoring of performance during this time is essential.

Performance criteria need to be set against which judgements are going to be made and staff development needs identified. Teaching staff should be observed, for example, at least twice in the classroom to make sure they really can teach and a checklist produced for each appointment that lists what constitutes a satisfactory completion of probation. A successful probationary period means that everyone is happy. The newcomer has integrated well and is making a full contribution to the progress of the organization. It is a part of the performance management process. If the individual doesn't meet the required standards, say goodbye as soon as you know it's not going to work and before the probation ends. The result of the probationary period should be pass or fail. A re-sit opportunity (i.e., more time) never works.

Setting targets

Having something to aim for is generally considered to be a positive feature for both individuals and groups in an organization – hence the increasing focus on targets and target setting. The concept of SMART targets (specific, measurable, achievable, relevant and timely) makes sense, but there can be a downside. Have you sorted out, for example, what happens if targets are not achieved? This could, of course, mean several things, including unrealistic expectations by the target setter as well as a lack of real effort to meet those targets by the person responsible for achieving them. Targets are best set in a dialogue and seen as things to be aimed for that are slightly out of reach. They give a focus and a direction – that's their real importance – not whether they are hit or not, which is more a reflection of the target-setting process and environmental factors. Supposing you as a chief executive are set a target of achieving a surplus of £100,000 a year by the corporation and you agree that this is realistic and achievable. What happens if something goes slightly off course and that target is going to be missed? Do you batten down the hatches, freeze orders and look for the odd redundancy to achieve the target or miss the target while maintaining the integrity of the organization and explain why? There's really only one sensible answer. Set targets for the reasons given above and discuss where the individual/group has come in relation to them at the end of the period to find out the reasons why they have been hit or under or over-achieved. The value is in the process – not the end result.

Performance appraisal

In the ideal world, performance appraisal would be welcomed by all those involved. After all, why would someone not appreciate the opportunity to discuss their work and have a dialogue as to how things might be even better? The reason, of course, is that in many cases this isn't what happens. With little or no training for either the appraiser or the appraisee and a lack of a clear structure and agreed information around which the appraisal will take place, what should be a valuable and valued exercise becomes at best a cosy chat or at worst a confrontation as to whose fault it was that x or y didn't happen.

As you will have gathered from the above, I am an advocate of both a college-wide structure for the appraisal interview and basic training for all those involved on what is expected to come from the appraisal event and the manner and spirit in which it should be conducted. I am also a believer in 360-degree appraisal, with 'upward' as well as 'downward' feedback. To make sure that appraisal takes place on a regular basis, you may wish to set an appraisal season (for example April–July), during which time the whole college takes part in the exercise. This can then be linked to the annual pay round (in many colleges from 1 August) with the satisfactory conclusion to the appraisal being the trigger for a pay rise to take place. There are cases where this has been introduced where the percentage of appraisals undertaken in a year has gone from less than 50 per cent to 100 per cent overnight.

An appraisal system is also strengthened if the appraisal 'paperwork' is not only signed off by the appraiser and appraisee but also passes up the line to a second-level reviewer. This aids consistency and gives the line manager's manager (the reviewer) an overview of their whole operation.

Staff development

You would think that organizations whose very reason for being is the provision of education and training to develop and improve performance through skill-enhancement would be paragons of virtue when it comes to the provision of staff development. Unfortunately this is not always the case. At worst, the staff development programme is little more than a series of course approvals, meeting the interests of proactive individuals; at best, it is a carefully conceived programme of various activities (e.g. work shadowing, industrial experience, internal and external secondments, as well as courses) that starts with the college's strategic plan, looks at what is present in the organization and the skills that are going to be needed and by whom to fulfil that plan, and marries this in with the needs/ wants of the individual. Planning and delivering staff development is a skilled activity and should start with the assumption that everyone and every college needs developing and that this development is a joint institution and individual responsibility.

The appraisal process has an important part to play in analysing present performance and present and future needs, but other parts of the quality-monitoring process are also likely to throw up needs that good staff development can help address. The teacher observation process, for example, will often lead to the identification of a number of common problems by the observers that may be addressed by providing specific coaching sessions (e.g. how to deal with late arrivals and problems of attendance) or by linking individuals with others in the college who are particularly good at dealing with these issues in order to learn from the experts.

Whatever else they are doing, all staff should be encouraged to 'get out more'. Colleges can become quite insular and a requirement, say, of five days' work experience or visits to other relevant organizations each year can benefit support staff as much as teachers. For all activities, make sure there is the opportunity for staff and line managers to comment on its usefulness and how it fits into what the organization is trying to achieve – ideally before and after the event. Where attendance at an external conference whose content may be of interest to

many is involved, ensure that there is a simple way of dis-
seminating the key messages (possibly through an online pro
forma) so that the pearls of wisdom do not remain locked in
one individual brain.

Think about your own staff development as well. As a leader
or manager, your needs are at least as great, or even greater,
than those of other staff. This doesn't necessarily mean lots of
time out of college on the conference circuit – a few days 'back
to the floor' where you undertake basic support or teaching
jobs might be an excellent way of improving your understanding of the organization, for example – or there may be
aspects of your skills that may be extended by online learning or
even by attending one of your own college's courses. But plan
what you are going to do and why – in the same way as you
would expect your staff to do.

Dismissals and redundancies

In the best of all possible worlds, of course, all staff would
perform wonderfully and adapt to changing circumstances so
that there was never the need for a dismissal or a redundancy. In
the real world, unfortunately, life isn't like that and, if you are a
college principal/chief executive, you will have to deal with
some major staffing issues, for example dismissing staff who
deserve to be dismissed and occasionally perhaps making staff
redundant for whom there is no longer a role. Neither task is
pleasant, but unfortunately they go with the territory. What's
important is that in these difficult circumstances, everything is
done properly, procedures are followed correctly and the
importance of the action to both the college and the individual
is reflected in the approach and resources devoted to it.

In cases of a potential dismissal, it is much easier to justify this
if there are basic building blocks in place which between them
provide a clear picture as to what is unacceptable to the organization. There should be a set of values that everyone can
understand, with perhaps a code of conduct describing appropriate and inappropriate behaviour (including, for example, an
explanation of what acceptable and unacceptable relationships
with students might be). A good college should also provide all

staff with clear job descriptions stating what is required of them and the general criteria against which their performance will be judged. Having up-to-date schemes of work, being punctual so that classes all start on time, teaching to an agreed standard and thoroughly marking and returning work promptly in line with a schedule are all reasonable demands of a teacher, for example, as would be the regular undertaking of staff development. Good record keeping by the personnel section, from the stage of job application onwards, is also important so that recurring problems (e.g. persistent absence) can be picked up and dealt with. Overall, if a dismissal is to take place, justice must not only be done but it must have been seen to be done. For that to happen there must be evidence that the individual has known what they should do but has failed to perform in their role, despite guidance and support. Otherwise, there will be difficulties in any ensuing tribunal.

The likelihood or possibility of a tribunal doesn't mean, of course, that problems should be avoided. Indeed, being too soft on a serious offence can often be as damaging to morale as a line which is perceived as being too tough. Ask yourself above all, when up against a tough decision such as this, 'Is what I'm proposing to do fair and in the best interests of the students?' Remember that, in the end, it is the good of the institution as a whole rather than the employment of a particular individual that is the most important.

Luckily, cases of gross incompetence or gross misconduct are relatively few and far between, but when they do occur, do not forget to hold a serious post mortem as to whether anything could have been done to have prevented the situation occurring. You may feel that this is a case of shutting the stable door after the horse has bolted, although in some cases, the stable may hold a small herd, rather than an individual animal.

Redundancies are, in my view, somewhat more difficult to justify and usually are at least partially the fault of senior managers not recognizing changing circumstances quickly enough or acting in time. It's very unfortunate for the foot soldier who has to be sacrificed because a general has made a mistake, and it is usually disastrous for morale. When faced with a potential redundancy problem, therefore, ways of avoidance should first be considered. Is retraining or redeployment a possibility? Will a delay enable natural wastage to deal with the situation? Are there opportunities for win-win situations (bringing forward the retirement of staff who would like to leave early, for example to reduce costs)? Are there temporary contracts that do not need to be renewed? Or are there other short-term opportunities for savings?

There will, of course, be situations in which, for whatever reason, none of these are possible – in which case it is paramount that the right people are made compulsorily redundant, not the wrong ones. The criteria for those who remain should be made clear. What skills and qualifications does the college need now and for the future, and who has those skills or, with appropriate development, could be trained to possess them? When you've addressed these questions, you need to turn the answers into a policy for selecting those who need to go. There may well be union pressures for 'last in first out', but rarely will this be in the long-term interests of the organization. Grasp the nettle now firmly or you'll end up being stung over and over again in the months or years to come.

Once the decisions have been taken, do what you can to support those whom you have displaced in finding a job elsewhere, providing extra opportunities and support for job searching and, if needs be, using the services of professional placement agencies. For long-serving staff, it is the least they can expect (remember it's probably not their fault) and how you deal with this problem will be remembered for a long time by those who remain.

Be aware, too, that in extreme cases of major redundancies, there may be a need for counselling for those who remain. They may be asking themselves, usually without justification, 'Why not me?' and be feeling guilty that they have 'got away with it' while their friends have not been so lucky. This is probably one of those times when you may need to go outside the college for additional expertise and help. After all, redundancies aren't a day-to-day occurrence – or, if they are, you really have got a problem and it's more likely that it's you and your senior managers who should be on their way. Whatever else you do, unless you're new to post and have inherited someone else's disaster, don't accept a pay rise in the next round. Remember the redundancies are really your fault.

Handling the good, the bad and the ugly

It goes without saying that every member of staff in an organization is an individual and as such there are as many individual relationships between staff and their manager as there are individuals. Characters differ and the way in which people respond to different 'stimuli' can vary widely. Some people like to be told 'how it is', for example; others prefer more subtle ways of hearing the same message.

For a leader and manager, it is important to remember that most of these relationships will be ongoing over a period of years – for better for worse, for richer for poorer, in sickness and in health, until a new job does us part. Hence any praise or criticism will be part and parcel of a developing 'whole' and should not be seen in isolation. Whatever is being discussed/praised/criticized, it should always be seen as a discussion/praise/criticism of the action – not the individual themselves, and the way should always be left open and prepared for the next relationship contact – good, bad or neutral.

Generally speaking, in all these circumstances honesty is generally the best policy – although remember that honesty can be delivered brutally or with a degree of subtlety. In the interests of the long-term nature of relationships, you should work on the latter. Look out, though, in particular, for opportunities to praise and give praise whenever and wherever it's due. Believe it or not, it makes it easier and more acceptable to criticize when things are not as they should be and builds up 'credits' for when something unsatisfactory arises. Remember too, that criticism is easier to take if it is followed by suggestions as to how the matter might be rectified, rather than a straight condemnation.

Do not expect problems to disappear or go away if you ignore them for long enough. If you are unfortunate enough to inherit someone who really came into teaching because of the long holidays and really wants to do as little as possible (i.e. they are lazy) don't expect them to have a Damascus moment on the way home one late (or early) afternoon. Tackle the problem as soon as it becomes apparent and worry it through to a solution. This may seem in some cases to be a disproportionate amount of effort for a manager to put in to solve one problem, but you must always be aware of the effects on your/their colleagues if you don't take the issue on. It's as much about encouraging others to perform properly and maintaining their performance as dealing with the reluctant individual.

Work things through in your mind before you tackle a difficult issue like this one and bank on opposition, often unreasonable, arising at every step of the way (that way you can only be pleasantly surprised if it doesn't happen). Most importantly, never ever back yourself into a corner with threats or ultimatums you can't or won't carry out. If you do find yourself in such an unfortunate situation, admit you are wrong and make sure that it never happens again.

On the whole, managers are better at dealing with problems than they are at delivering praise. Don't let this happen to you. Be aware of your CP ratio (criticism:praise ratio) and make sure it is at least 1:10. A good way of building this up is to look for opportunities to praise on your regular walkabouts (one principal I know aims for at least six every time he walks around and subtly transfers coins from one pocket to another, rather like a cricket umpire counting the number of balls bowled, as each is delivered).

Finally, if something looks if it could turn really ugly, go for outside help. There are times when expertise from outside should be brought in, especially when you are dealing with a rare occurrence or a one-off circumstance. It's far better to have alongside you someone for whom the situation is not unique than trying to grope your way on your own in unfamiliar territory towards your goal.

Dealing with students

We now come to the students. To what extent should you become involved with the 'customer?' This is clearly a matter for individual choice, but the numbers of students are such in an average college that regular day-to-day contact is not really possible, desirable as it may be. Perhaps the best you can hope for are 'tone-setting' meetings with students at the beginning of their programmes, supporting staff with difficult problems along the way and leading the awards events when success has been achieved. That, plus perhaps a focus group once a month, when coupled with attendance at the various student events that occur during the year, is probably as far as, realistically, you are able to go. It's really the job of the front-line staff (lecturers, course tutors, etc.) who will build up the real relationships. And never offer yourself for receiving custard pies or water sponges in the cause of charity at student events. Make a generous donation – you maintain the dignity of your office and avoid the bruises.

Dealing with everyone else

There is a priority list in some ways outlined above, but what do you do about the unsolicited phone calls and invitations that may flood on to your desk once you take up a senior post? Firstly, I suppose be aware of the part of the world you can and can't influence or control. Students (if they are indeed students) acting irresponsibly outside college in their own time is really something that you can't be expected to deal with – so don't get drawn in. Ask yourself, 'Is dealing with this really my job?' And if the answer is no – make sure it ends up where it belongs. Your job is big enough in itself without attempting the impossible of doing other people's. And remember, sometimes you are going to be faced with facts, not problems. Problems can be solved. Facts have to be lived with. Learn to distinguish between the two.

When the invitation is a positive one, remember that you can only spend your time doing one thing. Is it a good investment for you and the college? If the answer is yes, accept with enthusiasm. If no, apologize profusely and get on with the alternative.

9 Examining performance and improving quality

Determining where you are and benchmarking against best practice

Having been privileged to lead one of the country's best colleges for thirteen years, I have also had the opportunity to work for a while in a number of other colleges in the sector, sometimes in situations in which the overall quality had been judged to be poor and/or the college has been judged to be in need of recovery. In every single case, I have come across examples of good practice that were better than those found in the best.

All colleges, no matter what their overall reputation, have patches of excellence or demonstrate ideas and ways of working that are exceptional in the sector. For a leader or manager who wishes to lead a high-performing institution, the challenge is to find these examples from elsewhere and work out ways in which they can be incorporated into their own provision. For a manager of a curriculum or functional area, the task is essentially the same. Find the good ideas that are working elsewhere and steal them.

There are good sources of information in terms of each college's published inspection reports and a useful exercise for any area is to take all those with outstanding grades, read them carefully and pick out the areas of excellence that could be transferred or adopted. It is better still if the best of these can be followed up by a visit to see at first hand what is going particularly well. No matter how good you are, you can always be better and the secret of what to do next is often to follow those who have trodden the path successfully before. The starting point for improving quality is knowing where you are, what you do well and why others do some things better. For inward improvement, you need to be outward-looking.

Quality definitions

I've often heard it said 'Take care of the quality and the quantity will take care of itself', but what exactly is quality and how do you as a college leader and manager make sure that your institution is seen as one of the best?

These are not easy questions to answer. Quality is one of those funny things that you recognize when you see it, even though sometimes you're not quite sure why. It has many definitions with 'fit for purpose' or 'the meeting or exceeding of customer expectations' being the most common, neither of which are particularly helpful in creating an organization that is 'quality-centred'.

Quality control

To understand how the various components of a total quality strategy fit together, it is perhaps useful to consider a football analogy. Let's start with the referee (quality control). The referee is the person who decides whether or not the rules are being broken and, if they are, corrects the problem on the spot. In a college, your main quality-control function lies in how you deal with complaints. Even if you don't think something is going wrong, someone else does – and, in the spirit of 'the customer is always right', as a leader, you have to take complaints seriously and ensure that they are dealt with properly.

First and foremost, when receiving a complaint the starting point of your thinking should not be 'Is this complaint justified', but rather 'What do I need to do to satisfy the complainant and turn them from a critic to an advocate'? There is evidence to suggest that someone who has complained and has been satisfied with the response often goes out of their way to be positive about the organization to others. Similarly, an unsatisfied customer is likely to be almost as vocal and will tell others of their dissatisfaction. Whenever there is bad news to be spread, considerable damage can be done in a very short period of time. Providing refunds, letters of apology, discounts and complimentary vouchers to spend in the college restaurant are all useful ways to act in response to dissatisfied customers.

Actions will vary from college to college. What is important, however, is the approach. Complaints are free consultancy and should be considered on a regular basis by all senior managers under the heading 'What can we do to stop this happening again?'

Quality assurance

The next consideration is quality assurance. In football terms, the rules of the game – designed to stop things getting out of hand and hopefully preventing problems before they arise. It's the marking out of the pitch, the setting out of the goalposts, the offside rule, the definition of indirect and direct free kicks. In themselves, none of these will guarantee a good game of football, but the chances are that, if the rules are clear and applied, the results will be better than a kick about in the park.

For a college, the quality-assurance system is the systems and procedures that prevent things 'going wrong' in the first place and in an organization as complicated as a college there are a lot of these. How do you ensure that teaching is as good as it could be (the qualifications and experience of staff, the thoroughness of class preparation through schemes of work, the rigour of the teacher-observation process and its feedback)? How do you make sure that the right student is on the right course (admissions requirements, selection procedures, availability and accuracy of advice and guidance)? Or that budgets are not overspent (clear responsibilities, control mechanisms and monthly reports of actual and forecast expenditure)? Or knowing as soon as performance relating to key indicators deviates from its expected course?

In the best institutions, these and other key questions have been thought through and a quality or operations manual established which sets these rules and procedures down for all to see. This won't guarantee a quality college – but without it, a quality college is unlikely to emerge.

Quality improvement

The third element of a comprehensive approach to quality is a commitment to quality improvement and a system to ensure that this happens. Back to our football game, this is the individual player working on their skills and each part of the team working on their role in the overall performance (defence, midfield, attack). It's usually the result of hard work and training. In a college, it's no different. In a changing world, staff development for everyone needs to be seen as essential and ongoing. Everyone can always get better and this can be encouraged in a variety of ways, not least through the annual appraisal system when there should be a particular opportunity for the individual to demonstrate improvements they have made, say, over the past year and how they are now contributing more to the overall organization.

Quality management

With clear rules, skilled players and a good referee, you still may not have a winning team playing high-quality football. Someone has to decide the tactics – how the game is being played, what changes are necessary in personnel or approach, or where more practice or effort is needed. This brings us on to quality management. In football, this is a highly paid, though relatively insecure job, one person delivering a winning team or facing the axe. In colleges, the situation is by no means as clear cut. In some cases, the importance of quality, though recognized in the rhetoric, is almost invisible in the structure. There is perhaps one quality manager for the whole institution, usually devoted to the quality assurance side of the business. It almost goes without saying that quality has to be part of everybody's job, but managing it is a big job. My advice is to consider having a number of quality managers with responsibilities for various parts of the organization (finance, human resources, curriculum areas), with overall quality management also as a major responsibility of one of the senior management team to ensure coherence.

Quality desire

Good quality control, assurance, improvement and management – you have them all, but somehow you're still not where you feel you should be. Of course, this may be a matter of time. Good teams don't appear overnight, but it may also be because there is one additional aspect of quality that is rarely mentioned. Quality desire. You and your team have to have a hunger for it. Which football fan can't name a footballer or team that seems to have all the ingredients for success, but it just doesn't happen? For some reason they have highly paid players who seem to be going through the motions without producing the results. Can you inculcate that desire to the point where it becomes an obsession? Where everyone is proud of what they are achieving, but never complacent or satisfied, and always feeling that they could do better? Leading from the top, this is one of the most important messages that you must get across. Even being excellent or outstanding isn't good enough. Get this right and you could be the next England manager.

Self-assessment

One of the most important tasks that an organization can undertake on a regular (usually annual basis) is a detailed self-assessment of how the organization is doing in relation to its mission, vision, values and key strategic aims. Like many aspects of a college's activity, there is frequently as much to be gained by the process by which the final assessment or document is derived than in the output itself, and some time should be devoted to deciding the best way in which a comprehensive and thorough self-assessment report can be produced.

Generally speaking, those closest to the delivery of the product or service will be in the best position to determine the key strengths and weaknesses and what is needed to move that part of the organization forward. For them to do so, however, it is important that they are aware of the purpose of the process (i.e. to lead to opportunities for improvement) and do not feel threatened by producing an accurate assessment of how their part of the organization is performing – warts and all. The worst that can happen is for a false picture to be painted in which what is presented is what the provider believes the recipient would like to see, rather than what actually is.

It helps in this respect if a common template can be produced and as far as possible a number of quantitative performance indicators agreed by each part of the organization so that, at the very least, year-on-year comparisons can be made. In the best cases, cross-referencing to best practice elsewhere provides a focus for the type and improvements that may be needed. In the case of curriculum areas, for example, these may be fairly simple to determine: student numbers, retention, achievement and success rates, quality of teaching and learning as demonstrated by a teacher-observation process.

For cross-college areas, even counselling, it should also be possible to provide some hard facts without interfering with basic principles of confidentiality, e.g. number of presenting clients, types of problem covered, amount of help given (e.g. sessions delivered), etc. Hence, even support services such as finance and administration should be encouraged to think through the criteria by which they should be judged and to report back. This may take the form of a series of customer-

Figure 9 Can't we just concentrate on the benefits of the new fitness centre and forget about the exam results?

service standards and a report on how well they have been delivered.

Accuracy and relevance is also best achieved by taking time to define the appropriate area for which each formative self-assessment will be made. Looking at who outside the organization might also be interested in the self-assessment report can also be useful, since it always makes sense where possible to kill two birds with one stone. Curriculum analysis, for example, is perhaps best done by areas which are likely to be separately inspected, and subdivided by the areas in which they are likely to be examined. At present, this would be by considering each of five key questions. These are: How well do learners achieve? How effective are teaching, training and learning? How well do programmes and activities meet the needs and interests of learners? How well are learners guided and supported? and How effective are leadership and management in raising achievement and supporting all learners? In turn, these questions will be set within the context of *Every Child Matters* (DfES 2003).

One eye should also be kept on the purpose of the report – an analysis of how the section is currently performing, but, more importantly, a guide as to what needs to be done to move it forward. Ideally the responsibility for each subsection should rest with an appropriate manager, overseen by a relevant member of the senior management team and with the principal/chief executive or their representative bringing the diverse parts together into a seamless and comprehensive whole. Strengths and weaknesses should be clearly identified, with appropriate supporting evidence and in each case an action plan produced which is designed to improve on each. There should also be a number of areas identified for development.

You will note that the above proposal distinguishes between weaknesses and areas for development. A weakness is something which clearly should be eliminated at the first available opportunity (an analogy might be a leaking roof in a house – if it isn't corrected serious damage will be done). An area for development is one where some work, possibly a considerable amount of work, is needed but it won't be disastrous if it's not carried out immediately. (In the house analogy, it might be an outdated and tired bathroom. It's functional but by no means as good as it could be.)

A typical structure for a self-assessment report is likely to mirror the requirements of the outside world for monitoring and the internal structure of the college for delivery. The report will start with the position as stated in the previous self-assessment report and produce evidence as to what has happened with regard to the identified issues in the intervening period. It will outline the key performance indicators as they currently stand and how they compare with what has been presented previously. Reasons for deviations/changes will be identified and commented upon. The current situation will then be described with current strengths, weaknesses and areas for development evidenced and a proposed action plan to take these forward produced as a conclusion. This will form the starting point for the next self-assessment report and, when linked with the necessary actions identified in the strategic plan, will form the main part of the college's overall development plan for the year.

An external view, possibly from another college, as to the comprehensiveness and accuracy of the document may then be sought and the final document can then pass through the corporation as a key component of the college's operation.

Determining where you want to be and how to get there

Valuable as the self-assessment process may be, it has potentially one key weakness and that is its inward-looking nature. It is the college judging its own performance and mainly in the context of what has gone before. Apparently, excellent progress may not really be such if the starting point is below what is considered to be the norm elsewhere or if other colleges are clearly doing things better.

To move the college forward, the best self-assessment reports will include benchmarking information drawn from the 'best in class', derived either from nationally produced inspection or other statistical data, or by a process of visiting and investigative enquiry in colleges elsewhere. All managers should be aware of working in their own bubble and should see it as a key part of their responsibility to have an accurate view as to what is happening elsewhere in the sector and what being 'excellent' or even 'good' really means. Board members, in particular, are vulnerable in this respect and should ask themselves regularly 'How do we know that what the chief executive/senior management team are presenting to us really does demonstrate the excellence or relatively good performance that is claimed?' Honesty should be expected, but not relied upon.

Development plans

An organization that isn't going forward is probably going backwards. Hence there is the need for a development or improvement plan for a college to progress. This does not need to be a separately constructed document but, as I have indicated, can be a combination of the key actions for the future contained within the strategic plan and the action plan deriving from the self-assessment report. It should also of course take into account the development plans of other key stakeholders (e.g. the LSC).

For each development action, there should be a single named person whose responsibility it is to see that this action is delivered (if it falls across a number of areas, one person from those responsible for the component parts should still be given the lead and the overall responsibility to prevent something important falling between two stools – by tossing a coin if necessary). Contributing staff and their expected contribution can be identified separately. The clearer the action to be undertaken, the better. Each action in the plan should also include an answer to the question 'How will we know that this action has been successfully completed?' and an estimated time of completion. Finally, the way in which the actions are to be monitored (by whom and when) should be added.

Using the wonders of the spreadsheet sort function, each person can be given their individual responsibilities from wherever derived and these can be carried forward to the appropriate appraisal for discussion. This is also the time to look at each person's 'cut of the cake' and check with them that what is being asked is reasonable and deliverable. If the tasks are equitably distributed between people who have the power, skills and responsibility to achieve them, you're up and running!

10 Changing a culture

Recognizing the need for change

Picture the scene. There are three weeks before Christmas and an interim principal has been appointed to take over a college that is in serious trouble. The previous incumbent is on long-term sick leave, no accounts have been filed for five years and the funding body anticipate a debt to be repaid of well over a million pounds. The staff have been protesting about the poor senior management team and have even paraded with pictures of their heads on placards outside the main entrance. The building is cold and bare. There are few students in evidence and even fewer smiles on the faces of staff. The axe man cometh, they believe, prior to a merger with one of two possible neighbours. An inspection is looming with a poor result anticipated. The situation in college terms is probably as bad as it possibly can get.

Move on three weeks and it's the end of term staff Christmas party. The interim principal has been invited and as they enter the room halfway through the evening the music stops. A cheer goes up and the DJ announces 'Here's the person who has saved the college!' (Note the tense.) More cheers and the strains of Tina Turner ring out with 'Simply the Best'. Fanciful? Believe it or not it happened and not that long ago. Ridiculous? Yes and no. On the one hand, what had actually been delivered in that period of time was very limited, but it had been enough to change the whole outlook of the staff from gloom and doom to a belief in the future. The $64,000 question is 'How did it happen?'

An analysis of the key events of those three weeks in my view gives a good guide as to how to create a positive 'can do' culture, even when circumstances are dire. There were five major changes, which when coupled with a different communication strategy characterized by high visibility, started the turnaround into what is now a very successful institution.

Some of these changes can be traced to a full staff meeting which was called within a few days. The interim principal first of all set out the extent of the problem (far worse than most people were anticipating) – fully, honestly and openly. A few minutes were allowed for the anger and blame to fly around the room before an outline of how the problem was going to be addressed was outlined. A reassurance was then given that, if everyone agreed to work together and if they were flexible as to what they did, then no one would be made compulsorily redundant or would suffer a drop in salary. A few questions as to what this flexibility might entail (mainly redeployment to avoid the need for replacement posts), a few grumbles that people might have to move site (yes – but you can't have it all ways) but an acceptance that this was a small price to pay for the security offered (once again Maslow's hierarchy of needs). Finally, the way in which the task needed to be tackled was outlined, best illustrated by two slides of the words and phrases that the interim principal wanted to hear in the months to come (No problem! How can I help? It's my round.) and the phrases that they didn't want to hear (It's not my job! I haven't got the time. I've left my wallet at home.) – a value and tone-setting exercise.

The staff meeting also gave rise to the another key element – a clear understanding that the success or failure of the organization depended on everybody playing their part (there could be no passengers) and a simple challenge to see if those present were willing to take their share of the responsibility to solve the problem. All 376 staff on the payroll were asked to bring in a spare picture from home the next day and affix it to the otherwise bare corridor walls of the main building. It was suggested that the percentage out of 376 doing so probably represented the percentage chances of success. In two days time the results would be announced.

Two days later, the pictures were counted. There were over 400 (some people had brought two – just in case a colleague had forgotten) of all shapes and sizes and themes – reproductions of *The Haywain*, posters of Ferraris, the odd Picasso – you name it, the walls were adorned with it. Most importantly, everybody could see the results. The bare walls of the college, and more importantly the atmosphere, had been transformed, at no cost, within 48 hours. Above all it was apparent that everyone had contributed.

The next element related to a problem that cropped up with an anonymous letter pointing out some suspicions relating to the honesty of a senior member of staff. The matter was immediately and fully investigated and the member of staff was first suspended and later dismissed. It was a not an easy time, but the key message was that problems were going to be tackled and would not be brushed under the carpet as they had been previously.

The final piece of the jigsaw related to how the organization was going to be run. Following the old style in which there had been a 'locked away' senior management, the interim leader established a new means of operating in which they spent a lot of time walking, talking and listening. They also decided to take on a small amount of teaching – re-emphasizing the flexibility requirements and 'needs must' element presented at the staff meeting. A Christmas tree and decorations were bought for the entrance hall out of their personal funds (no accusations being risked of 'wasting money' when the college was so heavily in debt) and a 'best-decorated staffroom' competition set up, for which a champagne prize was similarly donated. This attracted over 25 entries including a full-size and very ornate chimney with a stuck Santa, needless to say from construction, and a light display that would have put Blackpool Illuminations to shame, from the electrical engineers. The message was that there was serious work to be done but people could have fun as well.

And to support these changes there were some new mechanics – relating in particular to communications. There were early-morning surgeries for anyone who wanted to attend to ask what was happening or what progress was being made, regular union discussions with 'What would you suggest?' type agendas, and of course the tightest of all budgetary controls with all orders being personally signed by the principal and all new posts/replacement posts immediately frozen.

Five key actions – the open and honest sharing of the main problems, the provision of security for the those supporting the necessary actions, a demonstration of what the staff could achieve by using the law of large numbers, the creation of confidence that the leader knew how to deal with difficult issues, and an operating style that encouraged involvement and fun. In turn these were supported by a communications system that enabled everyone to know what they wanted to know. The problem would take another year to solve, but people's outlooks had changed. The exclamation 'What a mess!' had been replaced by the exhortation 'Never mind the mess, let's sort it out'.

Deciding on what's needed

Not every situation is perhaps so easy to solve as the one outlined above (in some ways the bigger the crisis, the readier people are to change), but the basic principles remain the same. If things are not as you feel they should be, first stop the problem getting any worse by taking firm (and possibly personal) control; secondly, get to the bottom of exactly what the problem is; and thirdly spend some time finding out why the problem has arisen in the first place. If you are still not sure what to do, especially if you haven't come across similar situations before, why not try talking to someone in a similar role at another college? It will be time well spent. Fellow college principals and managers are invariably willing to help with ideas, suggestions and sometimes even solutions.

Removing barriers to change

Change, of course, is not always welcomed and, in less severe situations where you are merely looking to improve on where you are rather than dig the college out of a crisis, there may be some, possibly even considerable opposition, as to what you are trying to do. It's probably not a good idea in these circumstances to take the 'I'm the boss and I know best', or 'What I say goes' line but to get the opponents to spell out fully what their concerns are. Then address them one by one. The better you have thought through the issue yourself before going public, the less daunting these issues are likely to be and the more likely you are to be able to deal with those that remain. There is always a possibility, of course, that the opposition is right and you are wrong. Hence, the earlier advice never to back yourself into a corner, but to use a 'What if we did so and so' consultation scenario to refine the plan before it is unveiled.

Your aim should be to win the argument, at least with the majority. Even then there may be a pocket of opposition, in which case it is probably worth one-to-one or small-group discussions to determine why they haven't been won over. If possible, offer staff opportunities to go along with the solution without feeling that they are backing down. If you still can't persuade some staff to go along with your way of thinking and there's an element of sheer bloody-mindedness on their part that they don't want to change, then perhaps it is time to put your foot down, point them to the first line of their job description which should read 'To support at all times the college's aims and objectives' and politely tell them to get on with the job. You haven't the time to keep on arguing over one issue. As a last resort, you may even suggest that they might be better off working in an environment that more accurately reflects their views. The message simply may need to be 'Shut up or ship out'. There's nothing wrong with strong leadership when it's needed.

Determining the ground rules for action

There is of course the question as to when you personally need to become involved and when it can be left to others. This is of course a matter of judgement and will reflect the confidence or otherwise that you have in other people to deal with a situation within the mission/vision/values/aims/policies and procedures that have been set down. Generally though, if you haven't burdened yourself with daily 'must-dos', you can give major amounts of time to important issues as and when they arise. As a leader, it's your job to hold together the 'integral nature' of the institution – to be the guardian of the whole. An action or inaction becomes important if it threatens key aspects of this whole (decisions or actions perhaps that seem to be in conflict with one or more of the values). At times like these, it is up to you to bring people back to first principles and remind them of the basics – the prime importance of the students and the overall health of the college.

Figure 10 I think I'll leave you to sort this one out. I've got an important meeting to attend to.

What to control and what not to control

Your aim is not to control everything. In fact, your desired outcome is really to give individuals as much control as possible over their own actions, together with the responsibility that goes with that control, and the skills to be successful. Think of a group setting off in different vehicles aiming to holiday together in the South of France. There are of course advantages in everyone sticking together (support in the event of a break-down, for example), but does it matter if some people take a slightly different route, albeit going in the same direction and aiming for the same destination? There will be those who will enjoy detouring through Burgundy. Others may prefer to visit the cathedrals of Chartres or Reims, or meander through Paris. Everyone will have a better time if they can factor in elements of their own preferences, likes and dislikes, without detracting from progress towards the overall goal. They are also likely to be a lot happier, not only on the journey but when they arrive.

Conclusions

So you still want to do the job? What next?

So you're fired up and ready to go. You've learnt that being a good leader is really just common sense, being able to stand a little apart from the hurly-burly and keeping a firm grip on the bigger picture as you move towards turning your vision into reality. You've also realized, if you hadn't before, that running a college is a big job. Your common sense needs to be applied across finance, estates, human resources, curriculum, student support and many other areas. To be a good leader and senior manager, you need to have a good understanding of the mechanics of how each of these works. You don't need to be a qualified accountant, for example, but you need to know enough to be able to read and understand the college accounts and have a sensible discussion with the expert (the director of finance) as to the best way forward financially. (Incidentally, if you can argue with him or her with regard to deferred depreciation you really are doing well.) You need to understand what motivates people and, perhaps more importantly, what de-motivates them. You need to understand the curriculum and the different ways that learning can be delivered to meet present and future needs. You need to know what makes students want to study with you, what support they are likely to need and how you can present the college in a positive and exciting way.

What this book hopefully has done has whetted your appetite to go beyond these survival skills, with a foundation of practical advice on which to build your expertise. Working in a college is one of the best jobs in the world. Every year/term/month you are changing lives and changing them for the better as you give individuals more knowledge and skills and hence more choice over the way in which they live their lives. If once in a lifetime someone came up to you and said 'Thanks to you I am now doing things that I didn't dream I was capable of. You've changed my life', what an achievement that would be. In a college it's an everyday occurrence. Remember above everything else – you are the difference maker.

Bibliography

Armstrong, M. (2003), 9th edn, *A Handbook of Human Resource Management*, London: Kogan Page.

Bach, R. (2005 [1970]) *Jonathan Livingston Seagull*, London: Harper-Collins.

Collins, J. (2001) *Good to Great*, London: Random House.

Cox, D. and Fardon, M. (1997) *Management of Finance*, Worcester: Osborne Books.

Crawley, J. (2005) *In at the deep end: A survival guide for teachers in post-compulsory education*, London: David Fulton.

Department for Education and Skills (2002) *Success for All: Reforming Further Education and Training*, London: Stationery Office.

Department for Education and Skills (2003), *Every Child Matters*, London: Stationery Office.

Drucker, P. (2003) *The Essential Drucker*, London: HarperCollins.

Flood, P., MacCurtain, S. and West, M. (2001) *Effective Top Management Teams*, Dublin: Blackhall.

Foster, A. (2005) *Realising the potential: A review of the future role of further education colleges*, London: DFES.

Further Education National Training Organization (1999) *Standards for Teaching and Supporting Learning in England and Wales*, London: Fento.

Goleman, D. (2002) *The New Leaders*, London: Time Warner Paperbacks.

Hamel, G. and Prahalad, C.K. (1994) *Competing for the Future*, Boston, MA: Harvard Business School.

Handy, C. (2005 [1976]) *Understanding Organizations*, Harmondsworth: Penguin Books.

Harper, H. (1997) *Management in Further Education: Theory and Practice*, London: David Fulton.

Hay Group (2002) *Further Lessons of Leadership: How does Leadership in Further Education Compare to Industry*, London: Hay Group.

Heller, R. (2002) *Manager's Handbook*, London: Dorling Kindersley.

Jameson, J. (2005) *Leadership in Post Compulsory Education*, London: David Fulton.

Kotler, P. (2001) *Kotler on Marketing*, London: Simon & Schuster.

Learning and Skills Council (2001) *Strategic Plans, Including Financial forecasts and accommodation data 01/01*, Coventry: LSC.

Learning and Skills Council (2004) *Agenda for Change*, Coventry: LSC.

Maslow, A. (1987 [1954]) *Motivation and Personality*, Harlow: Longman.

Nolan Committee (1996) *First Report of the Committee on Standards in Public Life*, London: Stationery Office.

O'Connell, B. (2005) *Creating an Outstanding College*, Cheltenham: Nelson Thornes.

Office for Standards in Education (2004a) *Why Colleges Fail*, London: Ofsted.

Office for Standards in Education (2004b) *Why Colleges Succeed*, London: Ofsted.

Peters, T.J. (1989) *Thriving on Chaos: Handbook for a Management Revolution*, London: Pan Macmillan.

Peters T.J. and Waterman R.H. (2004 [1982]) *In Search of Excellence*, London: Profile Business.

Porter, M. (1985) *Competitive Advantage: Creating and sustaining superior performance*, London: Collier Macmillan.

Tomlinson Committee (2004) *Final Report of the Working Group on 14–19 Reform*, London: DfES.

Index